never

We watched Jessie show true compassion to other kids while she was in the middle of her own courageous battle against cancer. May her story inspire you to look beyond your own problems to care for those suffering around you.

RICK AND KAY WARREN, Saddleback Church

I'm very touched by Jessie's amazing courage and compassion. I hope people will read her story and spread her simple message: Never Ever Give Up!

CÉLINE DION, singer

I had the honor of meeting Jessie and stuffing JoyJars with her in her home. Her passion to help others was inspiring, and I'm confident it will inspire you to make your world a better place. Never Ever Give Up!

EVA LONGORIA, actress, humanitarian, and philanthropist

I've learned firsthand what it means to never ever give up in life. Jessie showed a lot of people how to live it while fighting cancer. I'm confident her story will motivate you to live life to the fullest every day.

BETHANY HAMILTON, author and subject of *Soul Surfer*, professional surfer

Jessie's message to Never Ever Give Up is one for all ages and inspires me to live each day with hope and strength. Let it inspire you to press on, no matter how big the challenge is, so you too can make the most out of each day, just like Jessie did.

COACH CHUCK PAGANO, head coach
of the Indianapolis Colts

Never Ever Give Up is a message of strength and perseverance which is so important to children fighting cancer but it also empowers professional athletes to reach deep and go for their goals. I challenge you to read this amazing book and apply it to your life. Let's make the world a better place, like Jessie did!

> TRENT DILFER, National Football League analyst for ESPN and Super Bowl XXXV champion

Never Ever Give Up inspires us to continue to fight, no matter what obstacles life brings us. It inspires me to get up when I fall!

> MATT LEINART, National Football League quarterback and Heisman Trophy winner

I have a Winston Churchill quote on a plaque in my room that reads, "Never, Never, Never Give Up." I now have a new mentor —Jessie Rees. Her fight, her heart, and her mantra "NEGU" have reinvigorated my soul. I have been a volunteer for the Brain Tumor Foundation for Children for more than a decade, trying to bring joy to kids with brain tumors. Now, Jessie, her story, and her JoyJars have not only renewed my spirit as a journalist but also filled my heart with even more inspiration to make a difference in children's lives. Thank you, Jessie, for reminding us how precious life is and how a humble and giving heart makes all the difference.

> KYRA PHILLIPS, correspondent for the CNN investigative and documentary units

Like Jessie, you have the power to make this world a better place. *Never Ever Give Up* will inspire you and challenge you to live life to the fullest, no matter what life throws at you.

> JASON MOTTE, Major League Baseball pitcher for the St. Louis Cardinals and childhood cancer advocate

never ever
give up

never ever give up

the inspiring story of Jessie and her JoyJars®

ERIK REES with JENNA GLATZER

ZONDERVAN

Never Ever Give Up
Copyright © 2014 by Erik Rees

This title is also available as a Zondervan ebook. Visit www.zondervan.com/ebooks.

Requests for information should be addressed to:
Zondervan, 3900 *Sparks Dr. SE, Grand Rapids, Michigan 49546*

Library of Congress Cataloging-in-Publication Data

Rees, Erik.
    Never ever give up : the inspiring story of Jessie Rees and her joyjars / Erik Rees
with Jenna Glatzer.
      pages cm
    Includes bibliographical references.
    ISBN 978-0-310-33760-7 (softcover)
    1. Rees, Jessica Joy, — Health. 2. Brain — Tumors — Patients — Biography.
    3. Cancer — Patients — California — Biography. I. Glatzer, Jenna. II. Title.
    RC280.B7R44 2014
    616.99′481 — dc23   2014009142

Published in association with the literary agency of Hidden Value Group, LLC, 1240 E. Ontario Ave., Ste. #102-148, Corona, CA 92881.

Cover design: Studio Gearbox
Cover photography: Rick Brotherton
Insert background photography: Shutterstock®
Insert photography: Unless otherwise indicated, provided by the Rees family
Interior design: Beth Shagene

First Printing July 2014 / Printed in the United States of America

To our sweet pea —
we miss you so much and think of you
countless times a day.
We miss your hugs, belly laughs, blue eyes,
tan skin, blonde hair, and amazing smile.
Your life ended way too soon, Jess,
but your story of hope, joy, and love will live on forever.
You taught us to live courageously,
love compassionately, and laugh constantly.
We will always share your story, spread your joy,
and do whatever it takes to fulfill your wish
so every kid fighting cancer
has the encouragement, resources,
and support to Never Ever Give Up!
We NEGU ... because of YOU!
XOXO,
Mommy & Daddy
P.S. We will see you in a "wink."

contents

the walk

It was unseasonably warm for February, even for California. The day was sunny and crisp, and we had a four-hour break during my older daughter's swimming competition, so my younger daughter asked me if we could go shopping. Naturally. Eleven-year-old Jessie loved to shop, and it had not escaped her that there was a candy store just a few blocks away. Fashion and sweets—combine those two things in a single day, and you could make her as happy as a wren in a birdbath.

I connected with my wife, Stacey—"Meet us for lunch after Shaya gets showered and dressed"—and then headed out for a walk with Jessie. It was something we did often, window-shopping and checking out the latest in preteen clothes and accessories. It was such a happy day, far too beautiful for me to suspect it would herald the worst trauma of our lives.

We were in Long Beach to cheer Shaya on in the Junior Olympics. All three of my kids had taken up swimming, originally to my dismay. I was more of a competitive team sports guy —in fact, I had coached their soccer teams until Shaya one day said she wasn't enjoying it very much and wanted to try another sport. I was hoping she'd say basketball. "Swimming," she said. Well, that left me right out. I hated the water, but my wife had been an All-American swimmer.

"Okay, sure."

Jessie and their younger brother, JT, joined as well because my wife couldn't imagine trying to drive three kids around to three different sports programs. They all joined the Mission Viejo Nadadores, a team with an impressive history. They'd been around since 1968 and won forty-seven national team championships and twenty Olympic medals. Because of our family involvement, Stacey even ended up working for the team three days a week as a bookkeeper.

After joining the team, Shaya became a terrific swimmer and was very competitive, whereas Jessie was more toward the middle of the pack and did it for the camaraderie. She made closer friends on the swim team than she did in school. That afternoon, though, she was not competing, and I had her all to myself.

As we passed a pet shop, we saw a little dog wearing a pink outfit with metal spikes in the window.

"Look, Daddy!" Jessie said with a grin. It was like a punk-rock Chihuahua.

We held hands as we crossed the streets, six or seven blocks. At one point, we stopped in at Jamba Juice for smoothies, and Jessie ordered the Razzmatazz. We turned left out of the building, and a group of about fifteen people was heading toward us because the traffic signal had just changed. It was too hard to get through the crowd side by side.

"Walk in front of me," I told her. "I'll stay right behind you."

She did, and then there was a long stretch of nothing much on our left side. Just a big brick building—a bank or something.

That's why it surprised me to see her staring at it. She was walking straight ahead, but her head was tilted to the side, seemingly looking and looking at this building.

"What are you looking at?" I asked her.

"I'm just walking, Daddy."

Huh. "Okay."

I continued watching her, and she kept her head at that same odd angle. I didn't say anything for a little while—until I couldn't understand it anymore. What was so interesting off to the left?

I pulled her aside into a parking area and stood right in front of her.

"Look at me," I said.

Her head was still tilted. I gently took her by the chin and straightened out her face.

"Do you see me?" I asked.

"Yeah, I see you."

"Okay. Keep your head just like that."

I stepped back a couple of steps.

"Do you still see me?"

"I see ... blurred."

"Okay. Stay like that."

I stepped back again, until I was about ten steps back from her.

"How about now?"

"I see you, Daddy. I see two of you."

"Really?"

"Yeah."

"Turn your head until you don't see two of me."

Slowly, she turned her head right back to that same odd angle again.

"Now I see just one of you."

"That's ... interesting. Okay."

When Jessie was in fourth grade, we had taken her for a routine eye exam where the optometrist told us she needed reading glasses and also had a bit of a lazy eye and needed help strengthening her eye muscles. We'd spent months doing "pencil push-ups," where she'd focus on the pencil's eraser as she gradually moved the pencil from arm's length all the way up to her nose and then back again to work the muscles. It had done a lot of good at the time. *Maybe we need to go back to doing that again*, I thought.

Despite the fact that she could sometimes be a bit of a drama queen, Jessie didn't seem particularly worried about seeing double. I was more alarmed than she was, but I didn't see a reason to get her nervous. Instead, we headed on to the candy store, where Jessie roamed around gleefully while I waited for Stacey for about twenty minutes. Then I texted her. "Something's wrong with Jessie's eyes. Where are you?"

"What are you talking about?" she wrote.

"Tilting her head sideways to look forward and says she's seeing double. Need you to see this."

"On our way."

Just because I figured it couldn't hurt, we did some of those pencil push-ups with Mentos in the store while we waited. I watched Jessie as covertly as I could—when she bent in to look at the jars of jelly beans, she kept her head straight. It was only when she backed up a little that she began tilting again.

Using a giant lollipop as a point of reference, I repeated my experiment when Stacey arrived.

"What do you see?" I asked Jessie, holding it close to her face.

"One lollipop," she answered.

Two steps back. Blurry. More steps back.

"Two lollipops," she said.

"Okay, tilt your head."

She did. "One lollipop."

Stacey and I exchanged looks, and then we put it aside and went to lunch, where I caught up with the latest exciting news about how the kids got to order room service in their hotel while I had spent the night back at home to take care of the dogs. Jessie loved staying in hotels, but in particular, she had a curious fascination with the miniature ketchup bottles and jellies and syrup that always came with room service trays.

As soon as we got back home to Orange County, Stacey scheduled Jessie's visit with the same optometrist we'd seen earlier. After an exam, he agreed that Jessie had some muscle weakening in her left eye—left lateral eye palsy, he called it—and sent us to an ophthalmologist and a doctor who specialized in eye muscle therapy.

She also had symptoms of a sinus infection, though, so the next stop was her pediatrician's office a few days later. In addition to giving us a prescription for antibiotics, Dr. Del Valle told us to go back to the optometrist to check out Jessie's bloodshot left eye.

The next two weeks were filled with doctor visits, one after another. The doctor didn't know why her eye was bloodshot but prescribed drops to relieve it. The specialist suggested a certain type of prism glasses to help correct Jessie's double vision.

"Has she had any other symptoms?" the specialist asked.

"Of what?"

"Just any other physical complaints or problems?"

"She's had headaches lately."

"Where?"

Jessie pointed to the back of her head, down by her neck. She had been complaining about headaches for a couple of weeks, about once a day.

"Let's do an MRI just to rule out all the bad things," the specialist said.

Once we were home, though, Stacey questioned that idea. "An MRI for an eleven-year-old? That sounds unnecessary. Let's talk to her pediatrician first."

But the pediatrician agreed. Of course it was probably just a weak eye muscle, but let's be *totally* sure.

It was with this sentiment that I prepared to leave for a training seminar in Fort Collins, Colorado. I was scheduled to go for a certification in organizational development consultation, to help organizations with their strategic planning. I liked learning and adding to my skill set, and I had been to several seminars like this through the years. We couldn't get the MRI scheduled before I left — it would happen during my trip.

"Do you want me to stay?" I asked.

"No, you go ahead," Stacey assured me. "I'll call if there's any problem."

Little did we know.

The MRI on March 2, 2011, was done in two parts — first a regular MRI, then one done with contrast dye. That meant Jessie had to be injected with a needle, which she absolutely hated. Abhorred. As soon as I heard about it, I felt guilty for being so far away instead of standing alongside her in the room to hold her hand. Daddies are supposed to do that when things get scary.

The technician told us the doctor would call with the results. I continued to take notes at the seminar and catch up with my friends, some of whom I hadn't seen in years. It was a fairly small group of us in the field, so we tended to run into each other at events like these and share experiences.

How nice it would be to rewind to that time, the last moments I'd ever live without the terrible knowledge that was on its way.

At about ten o'clock the following morning, Stacey sent a simple text: "Call me."

My heart jumped. She knew I was in the middle of the seminar, so she wouldn't ask me to call if it wasn't important. I excused myself and headed to the hallway.

"What's up, Stace?"

"They found something on the MRI," she said with panic in her voice.

"What did they say?"

"Dr. Del Valle called and said they found something on the film, but they don't know what it is yet and I have to bring Jessie to see a pediatric neurosurgeon at the hospital in an hour."

"Let's not think the worst. It's probably no big deal. Just a cyst or something. I'll get on the next plane home—just hang in there."

I really did believe it was just a cyst. Although something worse was in the back of my mind, I was more concerned about how they were doing emotionally than I was about the MRI. After all, Jessie was a kid. Kids aren't supposed to have real health problems. I just wanted to be there to hold their hands in case things got scary. *How would they remove a cyst?* I wondered. Probably with lasers—medical science had come so far so quickly.

I went back to the seminar to tell my colleagues why I was leaving. It was a Christian-based group, and they formed a circle to pray with me. Then my friend Bart drove me to the airport, where United Airlines got me booked on a flight right away. I had to rush to make it to the gate because the flight was ready to board.

Gate B-23. Gate B-23. Michael Jordan's number.

It's strange the things you think of at times like these. I thought it was a lucky number.

Stacey and I texted back and forth while I sped through the terminal and arrived at the gate. It was just past the appointment time, and this was the closest I could get to sitting in the waiting room with them.

What are you hearing at the hospital?

I don't know. I'm waiting to talk to the doctor.

A few minutes later, I'd try again.

Anything yet?

Not yet. Still waiting for the doctor.

First-class passengers boarded, and I was in the front of the coach line because I had "status" — a perk of being a frequent flier. And then, as I waited for the attendant to announce our boarding, the phone rang. As I answered it, all I could hear was my wife sobbing. She couldn't speak through the tears, so it took her a while to get words out.

"Honey, what's going on? I love you. I love you. Tell me what's happening," I said.

"Where are you?" she asked. Her voice was small and choked.

"I'm at the gate, just about to get on the plane. What's going on?"

"Jessie has a brain tumor."

No, I thought. *That can't be right.*

I searched for the right words to say — my wife and my children were more than a thousand miles away, and this was supposed to be just a cyst. This was supposed to be *nothing*, but it was a brain tumor?

Take it back, I wanted to say. *Our daughter can't have a brain tumor.*

It didn't make any sense. She was an athlete, a healthy little girl. Smart and good and careful. The kind of girl who follows all the rules. There was no brain cancer in our family history. This didn't add up. This could not be!

"I just spoke to the doctor," Stacey continued. "He says the tumor is in her brain stem—and it's not good. It's in a bad place."

"What does that mean?"

"It means it's inoperable."

"*What?*"

"He said we should just spend as much time with her as we can."

My first reaction was anger. *How dare this doctor tell my wife such a thing? What does he know, anyway?*

"Put him on the phone with me! I want to talk to this doctor," I said.

"He stepped out of the room."

"Honey, it's not true. We'll get another opinion. Listen to me—we're going to get through this. Where are you?"

"I'm in the conference room and I'm on the floor and I'm scared and I don't know what to do."

"Where's Jessie?"

"She's in the waiting room with Papa. She doesn't know yet. I don't know what to do …"

The sobs started again, breaking my heart to pieces with the knowledge that my wife was all alone on the cold floor of a hospital, and she had just been told our daughter had an inoperable brain tumor, and I could not get there fast enough.

"Okay, don't say anything to Jess yet. Wait until I'm there and we can talk to her together."

"She knows they found something, though."

"That's okay. We'll get a second opinion. We'll learn everything we can first, and we'll tell her together. Just stay calm and keep Jessie calm. I'm on my way, honey. I'm on my way."

It was a lot to ask, especially because I couldn't keep myself calm. As soon as I hung up, I lost all control right there in the boarding line. I sobbed and prayed, "Please heal my daughter," over and over.

I remember sending out frantic text messages to my family and friends asking them to please pray for Jessie. My whole body shook. Many of the people closest to me learned the news via a very blunt text message.

A few people got phone calls, including Jessie's great-aunt Marilyn (whom the kids called Tanta). She had known about the MRI and had checked in about it, so I called and told her that Jessie had a brain tumor. Then I couldn't speak anymore.

"Erik, are you all okay?"

"No," I told her, "I'm not okay. I'm in an airport in Colorado and I need to be home with my family."

I cried the entire plane ride, punctuated by frequent pauses to blow my nose, in the middle seat between two men. It was seat 7E, behind the bulkhead. Through my headphones, I listened to one of my favorite worship songs on repeat — Kari Jobe's "Healer." I must have listened to it fifty times: "You hold my every moment ... I trust in you ... you're my healer."

God, please heal my daughter.

It was frantic and desperate, the hardest prayer I'd ever prayed. I couldn't breathe, and time was not moving.

Please don't let this be true.

I sobbed until I felt dry heaves coming on, so I went to the bathroom to try to throw up, but I couldn't. I just cried out and prayed, and eventually I returned to my seat. Awkwardly, neither man next to me said a word to me the entire flight.

The moment we touched down, I called Stacey again. She

had arranged for a friend to pick up my car from the airport, and her father came to get me so I wouldn't have to drive. He told me they'd sent Jessie back to school so she'd have some semblance of normalcy while we figured out what to do next. She wanted to go because she had to take a test that day and was very focused on getting an A. On the way to school, Jessie had asked Stacey to quiz her.

I burst through the front door and saw several people already there to comfort us. It was good they had come, but all I wanted in that moment was to see my wife.

"Stacey? Where are you?" I called out.

She met me in the entranceway, and we just hugged and held each other. I greeted the others—my wife's family, our friends—and then I wanted information. I couldn't sit down; I gripped the kitchen chairs and stood on one side of the kitchen island while Stacey stood on the other, and I asked for every detail about what they knew so far.

Stacey handed me a piece of paper, and on it she had written the diagnosis the pediatric neurosurgeon had given her—pontine glioma

It felt so foreign, these two nasty little words. It didn't tell me anything. All I knew was that those words were my enemy.

"What can they do for her?" I asked.

Stacey looked at me and didn't say anything for a minute. It was like she was trying to soften what she had to tell me. "Honey, they can't do anything for her."

"What do you mean?"

"It's incurable. They said all we can do is palliative care."

"Are you telling me Jessie is going to die?"

"I don't know, honey. I don't know. They said ... twelve to eighteen months."

I pushed the chair away and walked over to my wife and we

hugged again, crying in each other's arms. I don't know how long we stood there, but when we finally let go, we saw that everyone else had left the room.

What do you do when someone puts an expiration date on your daughter's life?

When a child is diagnosed with cancer, it isn't just the child who suffers. It isn't just the parents or siblings either. Imagine how many people had to hear the news for the first time—her grandparents, aunts and uncles, best friend, cousins, teachers, classmates, swim friends, coaches. It was a devastating shock for so many people. I had texted my brother-in-law, Jessie's uncle T. I didn't know he was also in the Denver airport at the time. He had just gotten off a plane and was waiting to meet up with his wife, who was clearing security on her way to board a flight out to a training seminar. His phone's text tone announced my text: "Jessie has an inoperable brain tumor. Help."

He had to wait at the end of that concourse to deliver that news to his wife, Kim. Tenderhearted Kimmy, who has been so close to the kids since the time of their births. It was the hardest thing he had ever done.

All three of us had been at Denver International Airport, for three different reasons, when we got the news. All three of us have painful memories we can never erase. Kimmy broke down on that concourse, falling to the ground sobbing. They have to walk that concourse every time they travel.

Kimmy canceled her flight and instead flew straight out to us, with T following the next morning. Tanta, who was known in our family for her emotional sturdiness, went to pick up Kim at the airport. I didn't know that Tanta misunderstood what was happening. She heard "inoperable," but she didn't translate that to "incurable." She thought it just meant it would have to be taken care of with radiation instead. It wasn't until she and

Kim met with Stacey outside our house that the gravity of the situation set in — there was no hope aside from divine intervention. Every one of us believed in that possibility, so that's where our focus went.

My pastor, Rick Warren, arrived to join his wife, Kay, who was already with us. Pastor Rick had been a father figure to me since I arrived in his church in the early 1990s, newly married and looking for a place to belong. Since the church didn't have a group for young couples, I volunteered to start one and then was invited to work for the church in 1996. After attending seminary, I became a pastor at Saddleback.

Maybe people think that pastors are supposed to be "above" regular feelings like fear and grief, but it's not true. Even though I believed in heaven, I didn't want my daughter to go there anytime soon!

"Let's get on our knees and pray," Pastor Rick said, and we all did.

"God, please heal my daughter," I said — and I couldn't stop saying it. I just kept repeating it, loudly and painfully, an uncontrollable yelling. "Please heal my daughter! Please heal my daughter!"

I felt arms around me. "We're here for you," Pastor Rick said.

For about twenty minutes, I could do nothing else but yell and plead. Finally, Stacey gently reminded me that the kids would be home from school soon. We didn't want to cause alarm. Even though Jessie knew Pastor Rick and Kay from church, they weren't regular visitors at our house. She would know something was up, and we didn't have the answers yet. We had to ask everyone to go so we could clean ourselves up and try to act like our entire world hadn't just fallen apart.

The house was quiet for just a little while as the two of us struggled to swallow our emotions and bottle up our fears. Then Jessie came bounding through the garage door—she'd seen my car out front.

"Daddy!" she said. "You came home early."

"Yeah, honey," I said. "I wanted to be here with you. I know you had to go for that MRI yesterday."

"Did Mommy tell you I had to get a needle?"

"I heard."

When they got home, Shaya and JT went to swim practice, but we told Jess she didn't have to go if she didn't want to because of her headaches. She opted to stay home. In a way, that's what we were hoping because we wanted to tell her the news first, but in another way, it was terrifying. We barely understood what was happening ourselves, and we were falling apart—how were we going to tell Jessie just the right amount? The amount of truth that would bridge the gap between knowing nothing and knowing the abysmal everything.

Neither one of us remembers exactly how we ended up telling her. Those early days are such a blur of shock and survival. I know we said the doctors had found something wrong on her MRI and were going to have to treat it, but we didn't know how yet. Her eyes slowly filled with tears.

"But, honey, you're going to be okay. We're going to fight this thing, and we're going to get through this," I said.

What I didn't say out loud was, *"I hope."*

When the other kids got home, we ate dinner as a family like always, and then we had a family meeting. Telling Shaya and JT was nearly as hard as telling Jessie, because *they* deserved to still have hope too. Whereas Jessie would just accept whatever we told her, Shaya was fourteen years old and more likely to look things up on the Internet. We told them only the broad strokes of what was happening. We didn't use the word *cancer*, and we didn't tell them Jessie could die. We just said there was something in the back of her brain that didn't belong there, and that we were all going to have to pray as hard as we could because Jessie was in for a tough fight.

Nobody had a big reaction. Everyone was worried, but it seemed all the kids were looking to us for cues. When we assured them things would be okay, they believed us. Afterward, they did their homework and took showers. We watched television on the couch—Jessie's favorite part of the day—and we kissed them good night. Then Stacey and I went to our room and fell apart. That was going to be our routine nearly every night to come—hold it together until the kids were asleep.

* * *

The following morning, I had an appointment to see Dr. Loudon, the pediatric neurologist at Children's Hospital of Orange County (CHOC). I hated what he had told my wife, and I wanted to hear it for myself. If this man was going to say my daughter had no hope of survival, he was going to have to say it to my face. And Jeff's face too. Jeff Frum had been my best friend for fifteen years. Our families took vacations together, and we met for coffee before work every Monday. He was everything a best friend should be, which he proved again when he told me he thought he should come to the meeting that day. He had a medical background, for one thing, so he might be able to think of questions to ask that I wouldn't think of. And for another thing, he just didn't want me to be alone. Stacey wasn't up to hearing this doctor's harsh words again.

Meanwhile, I had put in calls to several other doctors for second (and third and fourth) opinions. While we were in the waiting room, I got a call from one of those doctors at the Children's Hospital of Los Angeles telling me he could see me that day, but only if I could get there in an hour. Jeff and I left Dr. Loudon's office—after all, we already knew his doomsday prognosis—and drove off in search of better news.

And we got it, at least potentially: The doctor told us that, based on what he was seeing on Jessie's MRI, there was a possibility the protein in her tumor was a different sort than the really "bad" kind. He ordered a more specialized MRI called an MRI-S, which we would have to wait to schedule until the following week. I pinned my hope to that—the "less bad" tumor.

On Monday, I went back to Dr. Loudon's office. Jeff had to work that day, so I was on my own.

"Twelve to eighteen months," the doctor told me, just like he had told Stacey. He showed me the MRI and explained not only that the tumor was in a terrible place—the pons, right in the middle of the brain stem—but also that it was interwoven with all the nerves, not like a separate little peanut they could neatly remove. There was no way to cut around all the tiny nerves to remove the tumor without severing the brain stem itself. Someone described it as grains of sand thrown into tall grass.

The doctor drew a chart on a piece of paper with a diagonal line. On one axis he wrote "Quality," and on the other he wrote "Quantity."

"Every decision you make from today onward will either affect her quality of life or quantity of life. It's up to you to choose," he said.

I wanted to tear his chart to pieces.

I spent the rest of the day sending out Jessie's files to doctors around the country. Someone had to tell me that this was a misdiagnosis, a simple mistake. Someone had to tell me this was *wrong* and my daughter was going to be okay.

No one did.

In fact, it was worse than just those two words—*pontine*

glioma. I don't know why it took this long, but we didn't hear the full diagnosis for five days. By that time, we had already gotten the results from the MRI-S and lost the gamble—it was not the "less bad" protein. I overnighted the films to a doctor at St. Jude, who added another two words. Now we knew that the proper name for Jessie's cancer was diffuse intrinsic pontine glioma, or DIPG for short.

It was the worst classification we could have received. In my research, I had found limited hope about cases of pontine gliomas, but not about cases of DIPG. DIPG was almost certainly a death sentence, and it was ruthless. I've seen it described as "a barbaric death." Because these types of tumors are located in the pons, they affect so much of a child's basic functioning. The pons controls things such as breathing, eye movement, arm and leg movement, swallowing, bladder control, and blood pressure, so all of these functions can go haywire when a tumor enters the scene.

Only about two hundred cases are diagnosed each year, which means there's very little research devoted to this type of cancer, and nothing promising on the horizon to do anything more than prolong life by a few months. A few months would not be enough. Didn't they realize Jessie had a whole life yet to live?

There was the smallest glimmer of hope—literally just a handful of cases where children who were diagnosed with DIPG were still alive many years later. They still had the tumors, but the tumors had not yet "activated" or grown. No one knew why. We wanted so badly to believe that Jessie would be one of those cases—that she would beat the odds. She would be in that less than 1 percent who lived, not the 99 percent who died. With all the people we had praying for us, God had to hear, and he was in the business of granting miracles. Surely she would be a good candidate for one of those miracles.

Dr. Loudon's eyes were firmly fixed on the medical books, though. He told us that without treatment Jessie would have just a few months left at best. That was never a serious consideration for us. We couldn't imagine not trying to fight this—and some of that was for selfish reasons. We didn't want to be without Jessie any sooner than we had to be, even if it meant she would have to deal with side effects from treatment. We also felt that the longer we could keep her alive, the more we could hold on to hope that a cure would be found.

The doctor advised us to see an oncologist to get Jessie started with a clinical trial, because it had been shown that radiation and chemotherapy could at least slow down the tumor before it grew. The danger of DIPG is that once it grows, it can't be stopped. The only hope is to shrink it or keep it stable for as long as possible—but normally, it grows within six to nine months after treatment, and then there's nothing more that can be done.

"I can't help her," he said. "You'll want to get started with palliative care as soon as possible."

The words "palliative care" sounded unthinkably cruel, like he'd just sworn at us. This was my daughter we were talking about. My daughter who had just competed in the breaststroke on her swimming team, who was sitting in her sixth-grade classroom right at that moment like every other kid, who had no idea there was a ticking time bomb in her body. She did not look like a dying girl. My child was strong and faithful and kind, and ... *why was this happening?*

It felt like standing on the tracks waiting for an oncoming train to hit us. That train was going to come; we just didn't know when.

"Will she suffer?" I asked the doctor.

"With this type of tumor, her physical suffering will be minimal. But her emotional suffering will be a direct correlation to what she sees when she looks in your eyes."

That haunted me. I already had in mind that I had to be strong for Jessie, but this made it so much more tangible: *My daughter will suffer if she sees my fear.* I practiced and practiced in the mirror, learning how to mask what I was feeling. Was she going to see through me?

Daddies are supposed to fix things. We're supposed to make the boo-boos go away. For the first time, there was nothing I could do to help my daughter. The train was coming right at her, and I was pretending we could hit the brakes. Cancer was going to steal a lot from my daughter, but I would not let it steal her hope.

becoming daddy

All I'd ever wanted, really, was to be a good dad. I didn't have much concept of what one would look like, but something in me wanted to right the wrongs of my own parents.

I was born in Spokane, Washington, and lived for a while in Moscow, Idaho, but I spent most of my childhood in Beaverton, Oregon. When I was eight years old and my brother was ten, our dad beat our mom so badly that we ran outside and hid under the car in fear. He had hit her before, of course, but this time was more brutal. She took off that day and didn't come back. She was a grocery checker at a local Safeway and couldn't afford to raise us, so she rented an apartment just a few miles away from our home. I couldn't blame her. She'd had enough of being beaten up.

That left me as my dad's stand-in punching bag, physically and emotionally.

My brother, Sean, was the smart one—the straight-A student who never veered from the straight and narrow path. He didn't waste his time with sports or girls. He was serious and had goals, and I was his fat little brother.

My nicknames growing up were Oompa Loompa and Little Porker. I didn't have many friends. My father would leave money for us on the counter to buy lunch at school, and instead I'd stop in a convenience store and buy junk—cookies, cakes, and candies. I tried to get kids to like me by becoming a playground candy dealer. I gave away lots of my haul in the hopes that they'd be less cruel.

At home, my father told me I'd never amount to anything and never be any good at reading and writing and math like my brother. He whipped me with his belt at the slightest provocation, just because he was drunk most of the time. He was a full-fledged alcoholic, and he also smoked a lot of dope. He'd get drunk and high and listen to opera music with his twenty-seven canaries, who'd chirp along.

I wondered if he really wanted us, but particularly me. Regularly, he'd tell us, "You can leave this house anytime you want. I'll even help you pack your bags." But I was a kid—a fat kid with few friends and no self-esteem. Where was I going to go? Who would want me? I wasn't even as good as that brother of mine, whom I resented. We even got into a few fistfights growing up.

One day, my father made pudding for dinner and topped it with Cool Whip, then left the house for a little while. I couldn't resist taking a swipe or two of the topping with my finger. When he returned, he drank for a while and then went to the kitchen for his dessert. Right away, he spotted the finger marks.

"Who did this?" he screamed. "Who put their hands in my Cool Whip?"

Sean looked baffled. "Not me," he said.

"Not me either," I said, trying to look equally baffled. I had learned that lying would sometimes get me out of a beating.

My father sat us both down at the kitchen table and told us

to put our hands on the table. Then he took an extension cord and cut off the end, exposing the wires inside. He stripped away the cord until there was a long length of wires showing, and then he plugged it in.

"Now, what I'm going to do here is I'm going to shock you until one of you tells me who put their hands in my Cool Whip."

Starting with me, of course. After all, the fat kid was the likelier culprit. He approached my hands with the wire, and I could hardly breathe. What would it feel like to get electrocuted? Just before he pressed down, I broke.

"Daddy, Daddy, it was me!" I said with tears in my eyes. I got a beating, but I didn't get electrocuted. I counted that as a positive.

I guess he had learned about electroshock in college. He had a doctorate in psychology and often reminded me, "I'm a *doctor*. You call me *Dr. Bill*." Not Daddy. Before we moved to Oregon, Dr. Bill taught human sexuality and psychology at the University of Idaho. He was the black sheep of his family—they were Mormon—and when we showed up at family reunions, they'd fight with him because he'd strayed from the church.

I don't know how far back his alcoholism goes, but I would guess his own upbringing didn't help. I later learned from his two brothers that when he was a child, his father would lock him out of the house and make him sleep on the porch by himself. As far back as I can remember, my father was a blackout alcoholic, and starting in the seventh grade, I wanted to learn what was so appealing about the stuff.

I knew how to make his 7 and 7s—whiskey and 7UP with three ice cubes—just the way he liked it. He would drink himself to unconsciousness, but he always made it to work the next day, so he was never forced to confront a "rock bottom."

Often, I'd wait for him to pass out, and then I'd start drinking whatever he had left. I'd steal marijuana from him too—not to smoke but to sell to other kids. My junior high years were a low point for me. I hung around with other kids who also had inactive parents, and we'd go to each other's houses and get an older sibling to buy us beer. We were the forgotten, the outcasts, the beat up and ignored. We drank because we thought we deserved to.

The summer between junior high and high school marked a big change for me. Even though I was two hundred pounds by then, I loved playing football and basketball, and I knew there were much harder rules when you got to high school sports. You had to exercise and do drills and pass "hell week," which I couldn't manage in my condition. So over that summer, I dropped thirty pounds and gained muscle. I learned for the first time to love exercise and to eat healthy. I did it for sports, but it had a side benefit too—girls began paying attention to me.

It was a huge difference, going from being a social pariah to suddenly being in high demand. I didn't handle it in the most gentlemanly fashion either, to my regret. I decided that if one girlfriend was good, then two or three girlfriends must be even better. I played the field and broke some hearts, and I never went back to being the fat kid again.

Because of my involvement in sports and my interest in cheerleaders, I followed the crowd to a group called the FCA —Fellowship of Christian Athletes. My friend's dad was the chaplain for the Portland Trail Blazers and also had these FCA meetings at his house, where kids who were interested in sports would get together and read devotionals and talk about faith. I'd never been exposed to any sort of religious teachings before. My dad didn't believe in anything. At first I wasn't sure I did either—I mostly went just for the opportunity to get away from my house and to hang out with my friends—but I know now

that seeds were planted in me back then. It would just take a few
more years for those seeds to germinate.

Soon came an even bigger change for me. My friend's parents
noticed the scars and whip marks on my legs and knew that my
father had inflicted them on me.

"We have to get you out of there," my friend's mom said
—and I happily agreed. Good to his word, my father packed up
my things in five big garbage bags and set them out on the curb.
I was sixteen, and my brother had just left for college. I went to
live with this family and got my first fresh start in life. No one
would ever hit me or beat me or whip me or scream at me again.
My sense of relief was enormous. It was as if I could breathe
for the first time in sixteen years—figuratively and literally. As
soon as my friend's mom got a whiff of all the smoke on my
clothing, which I'd just finished hanging in the closet, she said,
"Oh my gosh, we have to wash everything."

Each month, I paid a nominal amount of rent for the sense of
responsibility it would instill in me more than for the money it
would bring them. They were a nice couple, if a bit naive. Their
son and I would sneak out and get into trouble with regularity,
and all in all, it was much better than living at home. But there
were still bittersweet times, especially on holidays, when I felt
like a third wheel.

Why can't I have this with my family? I thought. There were
no good answers. My older brother was gone, and I rarely saw
my mother. My father—well, every now and then I still checked
in with him because even when someone does those things to
you, somewhere inside you still think, *He's my dad*. And despite
all the pain, there's still a little bit of love hidden deep somewhere, nearly impossible to extinguish completely.

After I graduated from high school in 1987 with not the
greatest of grades, I attended the local community college for

a year. Thankfully, my grades improved after that year and opened the door for me to go to Oregon State University. Unfortunately, I took full advantage of the Greek system and spent way too much time planning frat parties instead of studying. After two years of college, my grades still weren't the greatest, and I was not happy with the way my life was heading. So I reached out to my mom's mother and got another fresh start. I eventually put myself through college as a physical education major by working at a tuxedo shop in the mall on nights and weekends, and then by a combination of student loans and work as a personal trainer from my sophomore year onward.

My grades weren't terrific, and I was still a troublemaker most of that time, but I had the desire to be someone better. Not for my dad, but for me. I had already learned I would never be "good enough" for my dad—not even my brother was, in the end. Sean became an ER doctor, and my father still concluded it wasn't impressive enough. He thought my brother should be a different kind of doctor. I didn't have the same kinds of career ambitions my brother did, but what I had was a strong sense that something was missing. There was such a longing in me to be a family man. I wanted to be a young father and a good father, breaking the cycle of abuse that had defined my family.

May 18, 1990, marked the start of my dream come true. When I went in to interview for a position as a fitness director at a private club, I met the membership coordinator, Stacey Skeie. Her father owned the club. She had a warm smile, and we chatted and laughed while I waited for her dad. Immediately, I was smitten.

Stacey was a competitive triathlete. Once I started working at the club, I loved having someone to train with. I was competitive too, and we were well matched all around—aside from the fact that I had been in a lot more trouble than she ever had.

It took me six months to get rid of her pesky boyfriend so she could be smitten with me too.

As I got to know Stacey, I was drawn to her whole family. They had a togetherness I had always wanted. They were loving, giving, and fun—it was a completely different way of life and set of ethics from what I'd grown up with. Stacey wouldn't date me unless I went to church with her, though, so I agreed to give it a shot. At first, what appealed to me were the music and the sense of community. But three years later, on Father's Day in 1993, something deeper found its way into my heart.

Senior pastor Kenton Beshore at Mariners Church in Irvine said, "Even if you have no earthly father, you have a heavenly Father who loves you and accepts you for just who you are. If any of you just feel like it's time to come home, stand up and shout, 'Father, I want to come home!'"

Unexpectedly even to me, in front of three thousand people, including Stacey and her family, I stood up and shouted, "Father, I want to come home!"

I couldn't control the tears. An older woman on my right reached for my hand and offered her reassurance. I had just given my life to Jesus, and it felt amazing.

I was baptized shortly thereafter, and Stacey and I got married that August. We couldn't afford to stay in Newport, so we bought a home in Rancho Santa Margarita. Our loan officer told us about a nearby church that had no building yet—they just met in a tent. We loved it immediately.

That little church-in-a-tent became the megachurch Saddleback, led by Pastor Rick Warren. After a couple of years of volunteering, I was given the opportunity to come on staff and help people as the director of ministries—a coordinator who helped people identify their giftedness and passions and matched them up with appropriate volunteer opportunities within the church.

Soon after I started working there, in 1997, Stacey and I had our first child—a baby girl we named Shaya. It was the culmination of everything I'd been praying for—a wonderful wife, a job where I was helping people, a home of our own, and now a family. Meeting our baby for the first time was thrilling ... and I was scared half to death of completely messing her up. My mother-in-law stayed with us for the first week, and Stacey and I held each other and cried when she left. What were we supposed to do now? We were clueless and completely unsupervised! This new little human cried a lot, and we had no idea how to make her stop.

Of course, we eventually figured things out and managed to keep Shaya reasonably clean, fed, and happy. We loved her so much that we knew we wanted more children soon. We welcomed Jessica Joy to the family in 1999 and JT in 2002. Our family of five felt complete.

Every few years, we would make a trip to Oregon to see my side of the family. My mother was married to her second husband and still living in the same place. She'd had a stroke in 2002 and never fully recovered. Her memory was limited, and she was confined to a wheelchair. My brother married and also had three great kids we loved to visit. Sometimes we went to them, and sometimes they came to us. And yes, we stopped in to see my father too. Aside from that, when we talked with our kids about "family," we meant Stacey's side.

By the time JT was born, I had attended seminary and become ordained as a pastor. My role at Saddleback expanded, and I was now pastor of ministries, working alongside Rick Warren in many capacities and helping to organize the church's major events. The "pastor" title always felt a bit uncomfortable to me because it seemed to come with certain expectations. People expected pastors to know the Bible backward and forward, for one thing, and I didn't. My dyslexia gives me trouble with numbers, and the Bible is organized entirely by numbers—chapters and verses. People also expect us to have perfect faith.

My faith hadn't been strongly tested at that point. We had three healthy children, and about the worst thing that happened to any of them when they were young was the time when Jessie needed to have tubes put in her ears because of chronic ear infections. There were no broken bones, no serious illnesses, no car crashes or middle-of-the-night ER visits. I had no idea then how lucky we were.

Jessie's cancer was so out of the blue. It's the kind of thing that no family expects will ever happen to them, and it feels very rare—until you go through it and start hearing from others going through it too. Then it feels way too common. About one out of every three hundred kids will get some form of cancer before age twenty.* According to St. Baldrick's Foundation, more than 175,000 children are diagnosed globally each year.†
Cancer is such a terrible thing no matter what, but pediatric cancer is just unfathomable.

In those first few days, I read more about pediatric cancer than I ever wanted to know. It was haunting—stats and studies and personal blogs detailing the stages of treatment and progression of the disease.

Is this how it's going to happen for Jessie? I would think every time I read about a new and terrible side effect.

And why? "Why" was the other big question on all our minds. Why did Jessie get cancer? You think every stupid thought you

---

*See American Childhood Cancer Organization, "Childhood Cancer Statistics," www.acco.org/Information/AboutChildhoodCancer/Childhood CancerStatistics.aspx (accessed January 2, 2014).

†See St. Baldrick's Foundation, "Conquer Childhood Cancers," www .stbaldricks.org/ (accessed January 2, 2014).

can think at times like these, wanting to assign responsibility or blame somewhere. Was it my fault? Had I done something wrong to make God punish me? Surely it wasn't Jessie's fault, so what was it?

All I had asked for was to become a good father. God had blessed me three times over with beautiful children, and I had tried to live up to my end of the bargain by being present for them in ways my own father never was. I supported them, disciplined with love, tried to understand their individual needs and personalities. What Stacey and I had built was a loving and faithful family. Why would God let one of my children be harmed? I didn't have the answers, and it left my mind reeling. All I could do was pray for a miracle, and that's what I did, night and day. *Please, God, heal my daughter.*

how can we
help them?

If you have to get cancer, what you *don't* want to get is a rare cancer, because almost nobody is researching those to find cures. There's no profit in it. There have been great strides in breast cancer treatment because such a large percentage of research funding is devoted to it. Pediatric cancer research as a whole, however, is very much underfunded. The American Cancer Society spends just 1 percent of its annual public revenues funding research for all pediatric cancers combined. Now take into account that DIPG is rare even among pediatric cancers, and you can imagine how much money is being spent to find a cure: not much. What that translates to is that there has been no improvement in survival rates for kids with this cancer for thirty years, even though St. Jude and other research centers have been working on it all this time.

Jessie was unusual because she was eleven at the time of diagnosis, whereas most kids are five to nine. Over time, this would make us wonder how long she had had this tumor. When she went for that eye exam in the fourth grade and we ended up doing those pencil push-ups to strengthen her eye muscles—was that the tumor at work even back then? If so, she had already long outlived her life expectancy. Most kids with DIPG don't survive even a full year after it's discovered, and the two-year survival rate is less than 10 percent. The numbers beyond that are so small they're not even charted.

Symptoms of DIPG

There are few clear warning signs of DIPG, but they may include the following:*

- headaches (especially upon awakening)
- persistent hiccups
- muscle weakness on one side of the body
- clumsiness/difficulty walking

- difficulty swallowing
- personality changes
- hearing loss
- double vision/tilting head
- vomiting

---

*There may be just one or two of these signs before diagnosis.

The only real medical hope for us came in the form of three clinical studies in our state. Each study was slightly different, using different forms of chemotherapy combined with radiation. Once we had narrowed it down to those three, I left it up to Jessie to choose which of the studies she wanted to join—the one in Los Angeles, the one in San Francisco, or the one right near home in Orange County.

"If you choose San Francisco," I told her, "you would be away from the family, but either Mommy or I would always be with you. You'd stay in a hotel there with one of us during the week and come home on weekends."

"Can I shop while I'm there?" she asked.

Ah, Jessie. At least she was focusing on the important stuff.

We visited the children's hospital in Los Angeles first, and it was fine, but hospital-ish. Sterile. Then we went to the Children's Hospital of Orange County (CHOC), and Jessie marveled at the atmosphere in the radiation building. It was so serene, with waterfalls and beautiful artwork and soft lighting. Plus, they had trays of cookies.

"This is so much better than LA," Jessie said. "I want to go here!"

That was enough for us. We didn't need to visit San Francisco, because we agreed with our daughter. CHOC had a state-of-the-art facility and a terrific atmosphere, and we felt lucky it was so close to home. Of course, there were no easy decisions in cancer treatment. None of the centers could assure us they had even modest success rates—if success is measured in long-term survival. We had to have faith that we were making the best choice for us, and all three of us felt good both about the center and about the head oncologist, Dr. Shen.

Clinical trials are graded from one to three, depending on where they are in terms of progress and data. A phase one trial means it's untested, and they're essentially using patients as guinea pigs: How much of this chemo will be lethal? What will happen if we combine these two types of chemo?

Our trial was in phase two, which gave me a little more assurance. The treatment would entail thirty rounds of radiation, which would be done every weekday for six weeks at CHOC. Then there would be chemotherapy at home, administered orally by syringe. The medical team would treat any side effects that might occur.

Even as we were making all these plans and going for various tests and preparation work, I was still holding out hope for another answer. In total, I overnighted Jessie's files to forty doctors, including some recommended by my brother, Sean. My brother-in-law T's father was the head of oncology at UCLA, and his brother was an oncologist as well, so we were hoping they'd have more insight for us—something new that wasn't common knowledge yet. Something better than what we'd been told. Instead, they gently said the same thing to T: "Spend as much time with her as you can. Be there for the family. That's all you can do."

It was a shock to T, who had grown up hearing his father stay relentlessly optimistic about cancer patients. In his lifetime as an oncologist, the field had come so far! Whereas his patients' overall long-term survival rate when he started in the field was only 25 percent, now it was 75 percent. T's father had always believed in even the long-shot cases, saying, "If there's only a 1 percent survival rate and you're in that 1 percent, then it's a 100 percent survival rate for you." But now he wasn't offering any of his usual upbeat thoughts.

"Why are you saying this?" T asked his father. "I've never heard you talk like this."

"That's because there was always a chance before. But even with early diagnosis, with this type of brain cancer ..." He shook his head sadly.

I stayed up nights reading, but it was futile. There really weren't any secret answers hidden away somewhere. This was real, and it was happening to us right now. We couldn't spend weeks researching and making decisions. Once we had a diagnosis, it was just a matter of days before we had to commit to a course of action. It's difficult to think clearly when the mind is still in shock.

"You take care of the medical stuff; I'll take care of Jessie," Stacey told me. That was how our team operated. I was the one to speak with doctors and find out what to expect in terms of the progression of the disease, and Stacey would be the primary, day-to-day caregiver. She was such a nurturing mother and always knew just what Jessie needed, whether it was a kind word or a shoulder rub. I took a leave from work as well.

Even though I couldn't have had a better partner, the responsibility of being the medical liaison felt enormous. Each day, I sensed there were three sets of eyes looking at me, saying, "What do we do now, Daddy?" I wanted so much to have the right answers for them, even though I knew there were no answers.

It was important not to lie to them if they asked the direct questions. As a counselor had told me, if you assure your kids that nothing will go wrong and then it does, you've blown their trust. How would they ever believe you again? I did not tell them that the odds were severely stacked against Jessie, but I always left an opening—a "little chance" that the treatment wouldn't work. They didn't ask—and I didn't tell—what that would mean. I think we all knew. But there was really just one way to live—with hope. It was the only way I could imagine us getting through this. No matter what happened, we were going to wake up each morning with hope, and we would keep that hope tucked into our hearts.

The kids were close. Shaya and Jessie loved to dress up and dance and talk fashion together, and JT (who was nine) could still get Jessie to run around and play kid games with him. I knew what Jessie's treatments could entail. *How long will she be able to run around and keep up with JT?* I tried not to think about it.

We needed a game plan—some kind of order in the chaos. I told Jessie her treatment would have three stages: attack, battle, and trick. First, we would attack the tumor for six weeks with radiation rays, which would shrink it down. Then we'd battle the remaining tumor with chemotherapy. I even drew a cartoon-looking head on a napkin to show her what the brain stem looked like and how the radiation and chemo were going to knock out the cancer cells.

"Sometimes the chemotherapy stops working, though, which is why we might need to trick the tumor. We'd switch to a different kind of chemo or do more radiation to trick it into thinking everything is okay and it doesn't need to reproduce anymore, and we keep doing that until the tumor is gone."

She accepted my explanation without questions as I delivered it, just as I had practiced in the mirror—with the calm eyes, the confident eyes. I didn't ever want my daughter to have to look in my eyes and ask me, "Daddy, am I dying?"

* * *

Before the radiation could start, Jessie had to lie down on a table and let a doctor make a mask of her face during a simulated treatment—the day when they'd mark the spots to be radiated. We went for the simulation on March 11, 2011. The mask was made by heating up plastic mesh in almost-boiling water, then placing it on her face. As the plastic dried, it molded around the shape of her face and head, and then after a CT scan, the technicians marked the spots where the lasers needed to hit. From then on, the mask would be attached to the table with screws to keep her head perfectly still every time they did a radiation treatment —to make sure the beams hit exactly the right area every time. Even the slightest deviation would risk destroying healthy cells and allowing the tumor to grow.

Stacey and I weren't able to sit with her while she had her mask made, but we thought about her every second she was away from us. This was just the start of many trips to the radiation table, which she would have to face alone.

"How do you feel about everything?" I asked Jessie as we got back into the car to drive home.

"I'm scared about the mask," she said.

I didn't blame her. They told us that treatments could take thirty to forty minutes and she would have to lie on her back with her head pinned down to the table by the mask all that time.

"Well, there are lots of other kids there who've had the same thing done. Did you see the little kids? I bet it won't be bad once you've done it once."

"Yeah," she said quietly.

The three of us drifted off into our own thoughts for a moment, no one quite knowing how to handle small talk on such a weighty day. I started the engine and drove through the parking lot toward the exit, turning on the stereo to let the sounds of worship music fill the silence. We passed rows of windows—hundreds of kids in those rooms, all fighting cancer. Why were there so many of them? It wasn't right.

"When do the other kids get to go home?" Jessie asked.

"Some of them don't," I said. "It depends on the type of cancer they have and their treatment plan. The kids on the third floor have to stay for weeks or months at a time. Some of them have to stay in the hospital for their whole treatment."

Jessie was quiet for a minute, and then came her little voice from the backseat: "How can we help them?"

"What do you mean, hon?"

"They're going through a lot. What can we do for them?"

I looked over at my wife, who wiped a tear from her eye. There weren't any words.

We were battling cancer. I didn't even have any real concept that the earth was still rotating on its axis, let alone that other people still existed. My focus was entirely on my family and getting us through this fight. I thought it was sweet that Jessie was thinking of other kids—it was entirely her personality to do so—but I really just gave it a superficial acknowledgment at the time. I had no idea that those simple words of Jessie's were going to change the course of our family's life forever.

After we got home that day, Stacey and I retreated to the office to "check in," which would become our regular habit after doctor's appointments and treatments. We'd spend a few minutes with the door closed, discussing anything new the doctor had said and making sure we were on the same page. Stacey didn't want to know all the details I knew. She didn't like hearing the grim reality of what we were going to face in the future —she just wanted to stay in the present, love her kids, and deal with whatever needed handling today. I tried to live a month ahead of my family. I wanted to know exactly what the course of this disease looked like. Of course, there was no exact timetable, but I wanted the most detail I could get. What I discovered was that radiation would make the tumor temporarily swell, so her symptoms would actually get worse—and we'd have to counteract that with steroids, starting now.

Of course, steroids had a whole heap of side effects of their own, none of which sounded pleasant. Mood changes, weight gain, lethargy—the list went on—and parents who'd been there suggested giving kids on this steroid a rather wide berth. We prepared for the idea that our daughter might become angry and aggressive, and I mulled over how to tell her siblings to expect that response from her.

Then we went into the kitchen to prepare dinner, where we found Jessie sitting at the counter with about a dozen brown paper lunch bags laid out across the counter. She was decorating the bags with stickers, foam letters, and markers, writing things like "Get well soon," "Don't stop believing," and "Hope you're okay."

"Jess, what are you doing?"

"I'm making goodie bags," she said.

She looked up only briefly, then deposited one of her Beanie Babies into the bag she had just finished decorating. I looked at the pile of Beanie Babies next to her and realized she was about to give away her whole collection.

"You're serious about helping the other kids."

"Yes. Let's help them."

I scratched my head. I was a pastor. Helping was what I did, but I never pressured my kids to be extra charitable or "perfect." I didn't want my position to put higher expectations on them. Of course I wanted to rear loving and caring kids, but I also wanted to allow them the freedom to be kids. Here was Jessie, though, choosing to help those who were less fortunate, even when she was, to most others, the "less fortunate" herself.

"Okay," I said. "Just let me talk to the nurses tomorrow. I'm sure they could use toys, but I don't know if there are any rules about what you're allowed to bring in. Let's just ask first."

She agreed, but she kept going anyway, quietly determined. Just as she wasn't wasting much energy thinking about what might happen if the treatment didn't work, so she wasn't expending any energy worrying about the nurses saying no.

That night, Jessie felt lucky to be sleeping in her own bed. She had just learned that the kids on the third floor at CHOC weren't so lucky. They were in an unfamiliar place filled with monitors and bright lights and the smell of disinfectant, instead of experiencing the comfort of home with two dogs, two siblings, Mom and Dad, and their own fluffy blankets.

Life became so simple that day.

Jessie felt *lucky*. She was scared, but she'd already found a purpose. I decided to ride in her wake and feel lucky too. All of my family was together that night. We were all under the same roof, and we were all okay. From then on, life would always be that simple. Every day that Jessie was alive was a good day.

attack

Word about Jessie's cancer spread very quickly. As soon as Stacey called in to work the first day to say she couldn't come in, her coworkers at the Mission Viejo Nadadores swim team were fast to offer support. Pastor Rick alerted the staff at Saddleback, word trickled to the congregation, and Stacey spoke to Jessie's teacher and principal. We didn't have to cook for months. We received endless supplies of food, flowers, and presents on our doorstep. And there were phone calls and e-mails every day. My brother and I grew closer as he sent me videotaped messages every week asking about Jessie and telling me he loved me.

"Everybody wants to know how you're doing, Jess. We should start a CaringBridge page for you," I said one day.

"No!" she said definitively, and it took me a while to realize why she was so opposed to the idea. Over the years, particularly because of my role as a pastor at Saddleback, we'd often visited the website CaringBridge.org to read updates about people in our congregation with serious illnesses. Most often, they were older members, and their families wrote about their treatments

and their prayer requests. We'd sit as a family and pray for them
—but rarely did those people get *off* CaringBridge. Jessie associated the website with dying, and she was most emphatically
not dying.

"How about a Facebook page then?"

"I'm not thirteen."

Jessie played by the rules.

"It's okay, Jess. I'll take the heat if there's any trouble."

After a bit of convincing, she allowed me to set up a fan page
for her. I wanted a place where we could direct anyone who
wanted to support Jessie on this journey. It would be an easy
way to update lots of people at once rather than making dozens
of phone calls with news. She agreed because she thought it
would be a good way to ask people to donate toys for her goodie
bags—which we soon renamed.

A quick talk with the nurses confirmed that, no, they wouldn't
mind if we brought in toys for the other kids. They gave us a rea-
sonable list of what could not be included—food, sharp objects,
lotions, or choking hazards. Beanie Babies were A-OK, as long
as they were brand-new. Everything had to be new to make sure
it wasn't carrying germs.

So we had a family brainstorming session and decided we
needed something sturdier than paper bags to present these toys
to the kids. We thought that big plastic jars, like the kind used
for pretzels in the supermarket, would work best. And the name
we ending up choosing came from Jessie's middle name—Joy.
We would call them JoyJars®.

At a time when there was a lot of misery in our lives, I realized the value of having something positive to focus on. At first
I thought it was just for Jessie's benefit, but really, the JoyJars
helped all of us. They gave us something tangible to do beyond

just dwelling on blood scans and medications and scary side effects all day.

One of my closest friends, Rick Brotherton, is a talented graphic designer and marketing expert. We called on him for help, and he put his entire life on hold to make this happen for Jessie. Within days, he had designed a logo and started setting up websites. We put up a poll on Jessie's website to help us decide on color schemes for the labels on the jars. We went with the two winners—bright blue and yellow for boys, hot pink and yellow for girls. Then Rick made prototypes, and they looked terrific. Colorful and joyous, just like we wanted.

In the beginning, Jessie had both a blog and her Facebook page to update. The longer updates went on the blog, and the shorter ones on Facebook. Her first post was on March 16, less than two weeks after her diagnosis. In it, she told her "fans" that she was happy to have four days away from doctors. From then until her first radiation treatment, it was just going to be about family. Her beloved aunt Kimmy was coming for a visit from Denver, and we were all going to Shaya's big swim meet, where Jessie would proudly cheer her on.

By the time treatment day came on Monday, March 21, she already had more than one thousand Facebook fans. In five days! We were all amazed by how quickly it took off. Message after message said the same sort of thing: "You don't know me, but I saw your link on your teacher's page"—or a friend's mom's page, or a church member's page, or an uncle's coworker's page—"and I want you to know I'm praying for you."

One of those earliest commenters was Jax Shoults, a friend of Shaya's who said something that resonated with Jessie: "Never ever give up." Jess adopted it as her mantra, shortening it to NEGU®, which she always pronounced "knee-goo." When she went in for radiation, that was the phrase already on her mind.

The treatment itself wasn't the thing that scared her; it was the idea of being pinned to the table for thirty to forty minutes under that mask, unable to move an inch. The fear was alleviated only a bit by the idea that she could bring in her own music. Over the weekend, Jessie created a forty-minute playlist on her iPod Touch. She knew the length of each song and their order, so she would know just how much time had passed and how much time she had left before the treatment would be over. She filled the playlist with worship music that inspired her, like Kari Jobe's "Healer," Hillsong's "You Are Here (The Same Power)," and MercyMe's "Move."

That morning, she ate a bowl of Kix and took an oral dose of chemotherapy. Stacey gave her the medicine in a syringe. At nine o'clock, she had to go for blood work, and then at eleven, we sat in the waiting room until a nurse called her name.

"Jessica Rees?"

We walked Jessie as far as the door, but then with a kiss and a wave, she was gone. We sat back down in the waiting room and cried. It was all happening now. Our daughter was pinned to a table, having radiation to her brain, and we couldn't even be there to hold her hand. *She's scared*, I thought—and it broke me.

The minutes moved so slowly, and I didn't know how we were going to stand it for a half hour or more ... but then we didn't have to. After only ten minutes or so, a nurse came and told us Jessie's treatment was done and she was in a conference room waiting for Dr. Williams, who was overseeing her treatment.

"That's it?" I asked.

"That's it. You can come see her now."

We wiped our tears and shook out our emotions and quickly walked to our daughter. There she was, with a little smile on her face.

"I got through only two songs," she said.

"That was fast!" Stacey agreed. We hoped it wasn't a fluke, and it wasn't. For the next six weeks, Jessie had to go for radiation every weekday morning, for a total of thirty treatments. Each treatment ended up lasting about eight or nine minutes, with the longest one lasting eleven minutes. The doctor had decided that shorter, more intense treatments would be appropriate for Jessie.

After that first radiation, we went for Jamba Juice smoothies and then to the local mall for a Cinnabon—one of Jessie's favorite treats. She told us that radiation was a strange feeling, giving her a sensation of pressure in her head and ears, like her ears needed to pop but couldn't. There was a terrible smell coming from the ozone emissions when the radiation started, so we said we'd put mint ChapStick under her nose to camouflage that from now on. She also felt tired and unsteady on her feet afterward. The rest of the afternoon and night, she watched television and played games on her iPad.

On her second day of treatment, she got her own set of wheels. I was nervous about how she'd react, but she didn't mind much. The nurses introduced it well to her, saying that the wheelchair was around to help her if she ever felt like using it, because the treatments might make her wobbly for a little while. That's all it was to her—a temporary aid until she was healed. And they also said she should wear a mask in public for the rest of her treatment time to lessen the chance of picking up germs.

I saw the look on her face immediately. Jessie hated—*hated* —being stared at. She was the type who tried to draw as little attention to herself as possible. Even when roles were being assigned in the class play, she always asked for the smallest role so she could avoid the limelight.

"I'll wear a mask too," I assured her.

She grinned. "You're so silly, Daddy." Which also, of course, meant, "I love you."

Even though she was tired most of the time, she was also on steroids, which made it hard for her to sleep. The steroids were not the anabolic kind that some people use to bulk up their muscles; they were diabolic steroids, which are used to break down muscles. In this case, the steroids were meant to reduce the inflammation that the radiation would cause in the brain. The steroids would have just as many bad side effects as the radiation itself, but taking them was necessary to keep her brain functioning well.

The side effects came fast and furious. There were headaches, weakness, lack of appetite, and agitation first, along with the inability to sleep. She moved into our bedroom at night, and we bought audiobooks for her to listen to while everyone else was asleep. She listened to the whole Hunger Games trilogy in the wee hours, while also playing on her iPad. I'd sometimes wake up in the middle of the night and glance over to see if she was awake, which I could detect easily by the blue glow from the screen.

Once she fell asleep, she slept in later on the days she didn't have to be at the hospital early. We tried to get morning treatments to get them out of the way so she could relax at home afterward. She never went back to school, but we did pick up her schoolwork and have her work on it with her mom or Nana. On the three days a week Stacey worked as a bookkeeper for the Nadadores swim team, Nana would take over at our house, doing all sorts of lessons, from science to history. Jessie wanted to stay on track with her class so she wouldn't fall behind when it was time to go back to school. There were days when she was hurting too much to concentrate. On those days, she would lie down and Nana would rub her head, sometimes for hours. We were so lucky to have great support from such loving grandparents. I can't imagine going through this without their help.

Her fifth-grade teacher, Mrs. James, also stopped by to check on Jessie and work with her. Often, she would bring DVDs filled with sweet messages from the kids in class. Every so often, a DVD would show up on our front porch on just the right day —when Jessie needed a boost.

She kept an overall positive attitude, but there were still plenty of moments of frustration for her, like when she began losing control of the right side of her body. She tried to walk normally, but her right leg just wouldn't move.

"It's not listening to me!" she complained.

"That's because of the tumor swelling," I assured her. "It'll come back. You'll see."

She couldn't type. She'd sit in my lap and dictate to me when she wanted to write a new post on her website. It was a beautiful feeling having her sit there with me, but so sad too.

"We have to tell people you're typing this," she told me. So I ended the next post with "From Jessie's heart and Daddy's hands."

At the end of the first week of treatment, her biggest complaint was about her throat. She had a gagging sensation that wouldn't let up, and it made it difficult to swallow. She asked her NEGU Nation (one of her many nicknames for her Facebook fans—she also called them TeamNEGU and the NEGU Warriors) to pray for that feeling to end. Getting her to keep eating was a challenge, but I knew that sweets were the way to her heart. Unfortunately, the doctors said sweets were banned.

Banned?

Sugar, they explained, was no good for people with cancer. But, honestly, my daughter was facing severe life-or-death odds —going through awful side effects and doing it with as much grace as she could muster. I took her to Krispy Kreme to celebrate the end of her first week of treatment. It was the biggest smile I'd seen on her all week. There would be five more weeks of radiation and an undetermined length of chemotherapy, steroids, and other medications. I wanted to see that smile again. We would limit sweets, but not eliminate them.

I thought about that heart-wrenching "Quality" and "Quantity" chart of Dr. Loudon's and decided then and there not to sacrifice her quality of life, considering the odds that were stacked against her. I hoped and prayed for the best, but I still prepared for the worst. I didn't want to live with regrets if it turned out she didn't beat the odds.

A few local families chipped in to give us a wonderful opportunity to go to Disneyland for the weekend, and we gladly left that Friday. We didn't know what the future held in terms of side effects, and things were already going downhill so quickly that we decided to go sooner rather than later. It was an extended family trip—all of us, plus Nana and Papa and her beloved aunt Kimmy and uncle Tim. (She always called them "Kimmy" and "T"—they didn't like or need formalities.) Jessie needed to use a wheelchair, which was beneficial in that it allowed us to go to the front of the lines but detrimental in that she felt people were staring at her.

"Stand with me, Daddy," she said when we stopped to eat. "People are looking." She wanted me to block her with my body so people wouldn't look at her and wonder what was wrong.

Seeing her in a wheelchair was hard for Papa, who flashed to a memory of when Jessie was just six years old and we'd all made an overnight trip to Disneyland. Shortly after leaving the hotel on the way to Downtown Disney that day, Jessie had turned to him and said dramatically, "I'm just sooooo tired, Papa. I'm so tired of walking, and I don't know what to do."

"Would you like me to pick you up on my shoulders and carry you?"

"Oh, would you, Papa? Would you do that for me?"

In truth, she'd had more energy than any of us and probably hadn't needed any help at all, but she just loved to be held. Papa had picked her up on his shoulders and from her newly elevated view, she waved to everyone like a princess.

Now the weakness was real, and carrying her on his shoulders wouldn't solve anything.

Not only was she in a wheelchair at this point, but she also had to wear special eyeglasses and a mask for protection from germs. Because of the tumor's position, her left eye didn't close all the way and was always drying out. The doctor advised us to have her use an eye patch, but Jessie hated that. It got hot and felt strange. At night, she wore a sleep mask to block the light and keep in some of the moisture, and during the day, she had to wear the glasses to temper some of the eye problems. She still had double vision and dizziness because of the way she had to tilt her head to see straight, so the ophthalmologist said we could buy an expensive frosted lens, or we could just try Scotch-taping one of the lenses, which is what we ended up doing. I put Scotch tape over one side of the glass and cut it with an X-Acto knife. The idea was that her left eye wouldn't work so hard to focus and she could just use her right eye. She wore those glasses all the time and didn't mind them too much—except for the fact that they gave people one more thing to stare at.

The first night in Disney was fun. We had the Mickey Mouse suite at the Disneyland Hotel, which came with a round bed shaped like Minnie Mouse's head, and there were touches of Mickey everywhere—on the phone, carved into a cutout in the ceiling, etched into the mirror, on the wallpaper, and even on a sticker attached to the toilet paper. The kids loved it.

What Jessie loved most was the World of Color nighttime spectacular—a vivid water, light, and fire show where the characters are larger than life.

"Everyone should see this," she enthusiastically told me as we snapped pictures.

But on the second day, things got worse. Because Jessie had been sitting in a wheelchair for two days, Papa encouraged her to do leg extension exercises in the hotel that night. I deferred to him because he was the director of sports medicine at Orange Coast College. As she was doing the exercises, her muscles started cramping like a massive charley horse. This brought on waves of tears, and it became clear the first week of treatment was wearing Jessie down. The anxiety in the room increased, so my brother-in-law and I left for a short walk. It was so hard to see Jessie that upset, but it was clear this time she needed her mommy and Kimmy.

That was a terrible night, and one that started a tension in the family that I wish never existed. What I want to tell you is that we were the model family, going through the cancer journey holding hands and singing songs all the way. But that wouldn't be honest. What's honest is this: It challenged all of us. There were times when I didn't see eye to eye with Stacey or her family. It's easy enough to smile and nod when it's an acquaintance, but harder when it's your wife or extended family.

And believe me, I knew then and I know now that all they had in their hearts was love for Jessie. They wanted her to be cured, just like I wanted her to be cured, but we were slowly stepping on each other in the process, and I was the one who needed to be her dad. So that's what I told them. It was hard.

Nana and Papa were brought up in Christian households where faith was the answer to everything, and although they knew what the doctors had said about Jessie's prognosis and realized it was very serious, they just didn't want to accept that she might actually go to heaven. They understood she was in for a tough fight, but they believed she would win because she had Jesus on her side. When I talked about preparing for the worst, Papa and I didn't see things equally.

"You have to pray more," Papa told me. "God will heal Jessie. You just have to trust in him and have no doubt. You can't question him."

"Papa, it's God's will, not mine. And he may choose not to heal her on this earth. You have to be prepared for that."

"You're not trusting him enough! God promises us he will answer the prayers of the faithful—*anything* we ask in his name."

It was a little frustrating because it seemed to insinuate that if Jessie wasn't healed, it was because I wasn't praying enough. Not only was I praying with every breath, but I just don't believe in a God like that. I don't believe he punishes children because their parents haven't prayed enough. It was clearly the stress that was getting to both of us.

We didn't fight about it. It just hung there in the air above us, gray and thick. It changed things, putting up an invisible screen between us where none had been before.

We went back home to start the second week of treatment on an unsteady note. Jessie's side effects seemed to worsen by the day, and she spent a lot of time on the couch. At night, I had to carry her upstairs to bed and then back down again in the morning. We cleared off the kitchen counter to make JoyJars, which seemed to be one of the few things that cheered her up. We stuffed the jars with toys, crayons, activity books, funny socks, figurines—and when I say we stuffed them, we really stuffed them. "No air" was Jessie's first rule. She didn't want any space left in the jars. Her second rule was "no cheesy toys."

Most of the toys were inexpensive, but they had to be good quality and fun, not just "filler."

When we had finished a sizable batch, we took them to CHOC and gave them to the staff to hand out.

"Do you want to hand them out yourself?" one of the nurses asked Jessie.

I didn't even know we would have that opportunity, but Jessie wasn't ready for it that day. She wasn't in a great mood and wasn't feeling well. She shook her head.

"Okay, then, we'll give them out as we go on our rounds."

When we were ready to leave that afternoon, we walked down the hallway, and I noticed something. A little boy was sitting on his bed, opening the lid of his JoyJar.

"Jess, look!" I whispered. We walked slowly, nonchalantly. As we watched the boy open his jar, we saw a big smile spread across his face. We didn't know his name or what kind of cancer he was fighting, but his smile changed everything.

Jessie looked at me and smiled too, and for a moment, that was all that mattered. She had done what she set out to do. She had brought someone joy that day.

negu nation

Jessie did end up delivering JoyJars in person from time to time, always wearing a mask, which was required of visitors. She felt nervous walking into a new room, not wanting to bother anyone or obligate anyone to smile and make conversation when they might not be feeling well. The conversations were usually short. She'd walk in and say hello, wish them well, and tell them she had a JoyJar for them. Sometimes I'd offer to help the child open the jar. The parents asked questions and spoke more than the kids did, but that didn't mean the kids weren't paying attention. Jessie soon became a celebrity in the halls of CHOC. I would hear kids whispering to their parents, "There's Jessie!" as we walked past.

As usual, Jessie was uncomfortable with the personal attention, but she did love the reactions to the JoyJars. One mother came into the hallway with tears in her eyes, telling us how much it meant to her son. Cade was an adorable blond-haired little boy with glasses who also had a brain tumor and got his jar during chemotherapy. He and Jessie became "chemo buddies."

His mom, Erin, told us how adrift she felt. All of us parents, really, had that same glassy stare as we walked the halls of the hospital, always waiting on some test result to predict our children's future—whether they'd have many healthy years ahead or just days. She said getting the JoyJar felt like someone had reached out to offer her a glass of water as she was running a marathon.

It was a beautiful response that encouraged Jessie and me so much in reaffirming that what she was doing could make a real impact. Sure, it was just a jar full of toys, but it represented much more than that; it was a sign that they weren't alone, that someone was thinking of them, that we knew how hard it was to just be a kid and have some fun in these terrible circumstances. It was a get-well wish and a prayer for strength wrapped up in one. Most importantly, it was a reminder to Never Ever Give Up.

* * *

Jessie was not just a "giver of joy" at the time, but also a receiver. The reaction we got from people was astounding. Not a day went by that there weren't presents and cards on our front porch or flowers delivered to our home. As soon as word got out about Jessie's JoyJars, people wanted to know how they could help and donate toward the effort.

Three family friends—Sandra, Anne, and Bonnie, along with Bonnie's husband, Jeff, who helped with some painting—came to give Jessie's bedroom a makeover just in time for her twelfth birthday that April. They took down the loft bed that she now struggled to climb into and replaced the hot pink–themed linens with more restful lavender, blue, and sage green colors. Jessie loved the change. It felt not only more calming but also more mature for an older and wiser preteen.

Afterward, Jessie wanted to do something to thank the

woman who had organized the makeover, so we went to Build-A-Bear and made her a special bear that included a voice recording of Jessie saying, "I love you so much."

The day of her birthday party at the house was the first time she'd seen her friends since her diagnosis, and it proved difficult. You could tell the kids didn't quite know how to act around Jessie. I tried to explain it was only because they cared about her so much and wanted to understand more about how she was doing. Still, it was an awkward day, with no one really knowing what to say or whether to joke around as usual. Cancer isn't a normal topic of conversation for sixth graders.

Jessie retreated to the Internet after that for most of her social interactions. It was easier for her to communicate when she didn't have to feel self-conscious about the way she looked or the way people looked at her.

Every night around the dinner table for those first few weeks, we did check-ins to ask everyone how they were doing. JT always had the same answer: "I'm okay as long as Jessie's okay."

It was sweet, but it also worried me. What would happen if Jessie was not okay someday? She was his play buddy. He was nine years old then and in third grade, and he was always a handful of a kid—superhigh energy and funny. When he wanted to play with Legos or with his figurines, Jessie was almost always game to join him. They built "massive towns" together. He was worried about her and kept running over to give her hugs, which she would brush off— "JT, I'm *fine*. Cut it out."

Shaya was not as physical as JT. JT's love language was touch; hers was words of affirmation. They were both a strong source of support for Jessie in different ways.

After another day of presents arriving for Jessie, Shaya finally said, "I'm jealous." Her honesty was refreshing. The past month had been all about Jessie—every call, every piece of mail, every everything was focused on her, leaving the other two nearly invisible. After that, I had no problem telling our friends that if they wanted to bring something for Jessie, they should also bring a little something for Shaya and JT.

Some days Jessie said she was doing fine; some days she said the symptoms were really bothering her, or that she was just tired of all the treatments. And some days she just cried—and we cried with her.

"I hate that you're going through this," I'd say. "I'd do anything to take this away from you."

"I'll be okay," she said. She never wanted anybody else to feel bad. I couldn't help that sometimes Jess saw me cry. I held it together the best I could, but I was still her daddy and in a lot of pain. I'm thankful that God gave me the strength to navigate those days to the best of my ability.

On nights like that, we'd often find notes on our pillows from Jess. It's something all of our kids did, but Jessie in particular. She'd leave little love notes all over for us to find—in my briefcase, on the fridge, in Stacey's bag. They would range from sweet little missives filled with hearts and smiley faces to apologies when she'd been impatient with her brother or sister, but most of the time they were as simple as can be: "I love you, Mommy." "I love you, Daddy."

We didn't use the word *cancer* in our house. I know it may sound like a small distinction, but we used the word *tumor*, never cancer. To me, brain cancer sounded much more ominous, whereas tumor was just a "thing" that sounded more defeatable. So imagine my dismay when I found out that some of the moms from the girls' swim teams were organizing a swim-a-thon in Jessie's honor—with our blessing—and had sent out e-mails and made flyers asking people to come out and support Jessie in her fight against "brain cancer."

"No!" I said to Stacey. "It can't say that! Jessie can't see that."

Looking back now, I'm sure Jessie knew she had brain cancer, even in those early weeks. At the time, though, it was one of the few things I could control to lessen the blow for her. I had already given the doctors a list of words they must never use around Jessie—words like *incurable, inoperable, death, dying,* and, of course, *cancer.* I had also told them that any bad news had to be told to Stacey and me first so we could be the ones to tell Jessie. We didn't want anyone to be indelicate with her or frighten her.

The organizers of the event were so amazing and totally understood. They quickly redid all their flyers and posters to use the word *tumor* instead of *cancer* and to emphasize the positive instead of the negative. They did a remarkable job of putting together a major fund-raiser in just a few weeks. Three hundred swimmers showed up that day at a high school to swim laps to raise money for Jessie. In addition to the pledges they collected, they also held a bake sale and a craft sale, and sold T-shirts and swim caps that said "I NEGU for Jessie" or bore the NEGU logo. They sold out of both.

The mood was high that day as our family arrived and watched the kids splashing through the water, high-fiving each other, and mugging for the video camera. Jessie's friends taped messages of themselves saying, "We love you, Jessie!" and "We NEGU!" There were families there, with babies and grandparents.

All of this for my sweet pea, I thought. There is nothing like that kind of compassion to lift your spirits.

It was the day NEGU Nation came to life for us. These were many of her early Facebook fans, the same people who first cheered her on and prayed for her as she started treatment. They meant so much to her already, and seeing them show up in force was a needed burst of encouragement for Stacey and me.

Among the participants were five U.S. Olympic swimmers, which was a thrill for Jessie. Although she had to sit behind a table and wear a mask while she was at the event, she still got the chance to meet the Olympians and have them sign a sweatshirt for her and take pictures with her. For some of them, it wasn't a onetime thing either. It affected them more than I imagined, and one in particular, Kaitlin Sandeno, kept in touch with us online. The NEGU message resonated with her in her own life, and she looked at Jessie as an inspiration.

It was a beautiful experience for all of us. Jessie wasn't feeling well enough to stay the whole time, but we managed to stay for about an hour and soak in all the love and positive energy. The event was an astounding success, raising about $17,000.

We decided the gifts shouldn't go toward her medical expenses. We could handle those. This was Jessie's money to use as she wanted. And, of course, the first thing she wanted was to make more JoyJars.

She went onto the Oriental Trading website, known for its inexpensive bulk items for kids' crafts, toys, and party favors, and began ordering. Bouncy balls, bendable animals, rubber duckies — boy, did she love those rubber duckies.

It took some convincing to get her to spend some of the money on herself, but once I set her loose in the mall, she happily spent afternoons looking through scarves, necklaces, and hats. She and Shaya liked to put on fashion shows for us, modeling their latest styles to tunes like Beyoncé's "Single Ladies." It was one of their favorite things to do at Nana and Papa's house too. They'd play dress-up with whatever they could find. They were very lucky that JT was a good sport, because they'd dress him up too, and the dress-up clothes didn't actually include any *boy* clothing.

Jessie's strength varied from day to day. Sometimes she got around reasonably well, and other times she felt weak and clumsy. We tried to keep her moving for fear that if she sat for too long, she'd lose the muscle tone she had left. She loved being in water, so most of her exercise was in the Jacuzzi or pool, where she'd walk or swim around as much as she was able. The treatments made her cold, so she liked being out in the sun, even though she had to keep her skin protected from direct sunlight.

It was very hard watching my strong little athlete wither. She'd had a solid swimmer's body at the start of treatment, and after a month, all the definition was gone. Her muscles were broken down, and her whole frame looked frail. Most people on steroids gain weight, but Jessie lost weight. The only place she got bigger was around her face, where she got the dreaded "moon face" she hated so much — the swollen, rounded cheeks and jaw that distorted her appearance. That's common for people on long-term steroids. Her face was so puffy that she would emerge from radiation with circular indents all over it from the mask, which was now too tight.

I pictured her gaining everything back, from her muscles to her eyesight. I couldn't dwell on what was, but only on what might be. I clung to that 1 percent chance for all it was worth, believing that if anyone had a chance, Jessie did.

My faith tells me that God is in the business of granting miracles and that prayers do matter, and I knew we had thousands of people praying for Jessie. More posted prayers every day online too, as people read about her story.

That's all Stacey wanted to know about. She was not in any denial of the grim prognosis. She just chose to live in the moment. I kept reading about the progression of DIPG, reading the latest research, finding out about what symptoms to expect when the tumor grew and what side effects some medications might have. I focused on the doctors and the insurance company, while Stacey focused on loving her daughter with all she had. We both continued to pray and ask God to heal our sweet pea.

We both had our own sources of escape too. Stacey had close girlfriends who would sometimes go out to dinner with her or come by to visit. One of her friends even did physical therapy with Jessie. My main outlet was exercise. For an hour a day, I went to the gym and listened to music on my headphones and sorted out the thoughts running through my mind while I ran, biked, and trained.

I listened to the same mix of music as Jessie did during her radiation treatments. Several of the songs took on a personal meaning for me, and I even found myself inserting Jessie's name into a song like Hillsong's "You Are Here (The Same Power)": "The same power that conquered the grave lives in *Jessie*, lives in *Jessie*."

I didn't talk to people at the gym, and sometimes I cried. It was a time to focus my energy, to talk to God. I envisioned my child as powerful and whole, and I tried to get the images of what her last days might look like out of my head.

Because I did go there.

I was obsessed with staying two months ahead. I knew which symptoms typically happened at which stages, and I knew that the moment the tumor started growing after radiation ended, we were going to be in trouble. All the limited reports about DIPG were uniformly awful in their description of the last stages. During the last four to eight weeks of her life, she would completely break down. As the tumor grew, it would press down on the nerves in her brain stem and cut off functioning of many systems. She would lose the ability to walk and lose control of her arms and hands. She wouldn't be able to swallow and would most likely drool excessively—but there was a spray we could get to help dry that up. It seemed of little consolation. Because she wouldn't be able to swallow, she'd have to be fed through a tube that went down her nose and into her stomach. Most likely, she'd lose the ability to go to the bathroom and might have to wear diapers. Seizures would be common. Her eyes would not close fully. One mother described her son's descent, saying that by the end he could communicate only by blinking.

I pictured what it would look like at the end with my daughter lying in her bed, essentially an infant again. I imagined how awful it would be if she were locked into a nonfunctioning body, unable to communicate to let us know what she was feeling or thinking. What if she could still think clearly and was aware of the complete breakdown of her body? Would she be scared? Would I be able to look at her without falling apart?

Presumably, doctors would give her morphine or other medications that managed her pain and reduced her awareness, but even the thought of that was heartbreaking. I read stories of parents who kept vigil by their children's bedside for weeks on end, hoping for a breakthrough of some kind, but their children were essentially comatose and losing all bodily control.

Yes, I studied those warning signs of "the end," all the while praying for a miracle.

I was on leave from work during this time, but I went back because of Jessie. In the second month of her treatment, she just looked at me one day and said, "Aren't you going to go back to work now?"

It was a tricky question. What it meant was, "Why *aren't* you working? You've told me that everything is going to be okay, so why are you hovering around here as if it's not?" She wanted a sense of normalcy, and the fact that I was not working made her suspicious. Again, she was looking to me to gauge how serious this all was. I ended my leave.

I had many responsibilities in my role at Saddleback, including fulfilling a commitment each leadership team member makes to participate in an annual mission trip lasting at least two weeks. There were two main reasons: first, to keep our worldview alive and be compassionate helpers to people in need all over the world, and second, to help train church leaders wherever we went.

While those trips were enlightening, they were also difficult. It sometimes felt as if we could never make enough of a difference to be meaningful. There we were in the world's forgotten cities where residents didn't have clean water, let alone proper nutrition or clothing. It was hard to face these realities—and to be away from my family for that much time.

Each time I went, the kids would tuck something of theirs into my suitcase for me to find when I got to my destination, and we would have nightly calls by Skype, regardless of time differences. Shaya and Jessie usually left Beanie Babies and other little stuffed animals. JT was really into Power Rangers, so he'd put one of his figurines into my suitcase and then get a big kick out of seeing it in Tokyo or wherever I was. We'd play-fight with the figurines over the webcams. And I always brought home souvenirs—a Nativity set from Rwanda, dresses from India. Of course, I hadn't been expected to go on any trips after Jessie's diagnosis. They understood that I couldn't travel at a time like this.

One afternoon, I was called on to minister to a family who had just lost a child to cancer. I didn't know how I would do it, and the Saddleback staff told me I didn't have to be the one to do it if it felt too close to home. It *was* too close to home, but I did it anyway. I talked to Jessie about it first.

"What do I tell these people?" I asked her.

"Just tell them that he's on a mission trip to heaven and they'll see him again."

"What?"

"When you'd go on mission trips, we wouldn't see you for a while, but then you'd come home. His mission trip is in heaven, but they'll get to see him when they go to heaven too."

My heart broke and was uplifted all at once. Jessie's faith was strong, always. She believed in eternal life, and she believed that God was with all of us all the time. It was so simple in her mind. She didn't question whether or not heaven was real. It was. She was sure.

Did she know then that there was a chance she would follow this little boy to heaven? She didn't say. I tried so hard to walk the right line with my family. I never lied to them outright, but I significantly bent the odds in our favor. I always told them there was a small chance the treatment wouldn't work. What that meant, they didn't ask, but as far as I could tell, it wasn't something any of them thought about very much.

In April, Jessie posted this: "My buddy Jax came today to visit. She brought this cool poster that was signed by the entire Santa Margarita High School swim team. That is where I'm going to go to high school."

High school was more than three years away. She didn't question whether or not she'd make it that far.

But she did talk about her symptoms and her frustrations. "I feel lonely and limited," she said. There were days it got exhausting just to deal with the medical routine. She was on ten different medications when she started treatment, and then several more were added to combat the side effects of those original medications. When Stacey gave Jessie her chemo, she had to wear gloves to mix it and fill the syringe. There was something so awful about those precautions—the idea that you needed to wear gloves, the knowledge that no one could be near the radiation machine that was zapping Jessie every day. My daughter's body was being filled with poison that was too dangerous to be around unless there was something even *more* dangerous already in your body.

These were things too adult for children to consider, but we adults were unsettled. It would have been easier if everyone could have just had the same simple faith Jessie had that Jesus would take care of this and she would soon be back in school.

I'm sure that's part of what was on Uncle T's mind when he surprised me and asked, "Would you baptize me?" He was not one to be vocal about his faith, so it caught me off guard.

"My gosh, Tim," I said. "I'd be honored."

"But I don't want to do it in church. Can we do it at your house or something?"

We decided on our backyard Jacuzzi, and then T did something that will stay with me forever. He asked Jessie if she wanted to be baptized with him.

They shared such a special bond, and Jessie was excited to say yes. She had already given her heart to Jesus years earlier and had taken classes at Saddleback, so she knew the meaning of baptism. It's not a requirement to go to heaven, and in the Southern Baptist tradition, it has to be done on each person's own terms—meaning there's no set schedule for when a person should be baptized. This was the right time for both of them. JT asked if he could be baptized too. He had recently taken his preparation classes, so I agreed.

It was just family in the backyard, and Rick Brotherton, though he qualifies as family too. Rick was there to take pictures. Without us having to discuss these things, Rick just knew the gravity of days like this. We needed these pictures — for someday.

I had baptized several hundred people at Saddleback, but never my own family members. First I baptized Tim, then JT. Jessie needed help getting into the water because she was unsteady on her feet. Kim and T helped her to the side of the Jacuzzi, and then I held her arms and eased her into the water and stood with her in the middle.

"Jessie, have you accepted Jesus to be your Lord and Savior?" I asked.

"Yes," she said.

"Is it your plan to follow him to the best of your ability every day of your life?"

"Yes."

"Okay. Because of your profession of faith in front of Mommy, Shaya, JT, Kimmy, T, Nana, and Papa — go ahead and cross your arms, and you can hold your nose if you want to — it's my honor to baptize you, my daughter."

I dunked her into the water as I said, "Buried with Christ in baptism," then pulled her up as I said, "Raised to walk in new life."

It was one of the most meaningful moments of my life, and hers.

Jessie took her faith seriously, and each night she would sit on the bathroom floor with Stacey and read from her devotional book in search of guidance to bring her closer to God. It was something she had decided to do after her diagnosis, and she particularly liked a book called *Chick Chat: More Devotions for Girls* by Kristi Holl. One night, the lesson was about doing your best for the Lord, no matter what the task, and she said, "I don't want to go to treatment tomorrow, but I'm going to be in a good mood for God."

She shared some of these devotionals with her NEGU Nation online. Jessie was not preachy, but she shared her faith in the innocent way children do best—living by example. When she talked about a devotional about forgiveness, she said that sometimes she was short with her brother and needed to ask God for forgiveness for that. She was thankful that God blots out her sins and doesn't keep a log of them.

We have always made sure our children know they can trust God, no matter how bad things look. God is our source of hope, strength, and power, and one of our family mottos is "Hold on to God and hold on to each other."

When she was up to typing on her own again, Jessie discovered she could find prayer requests by using the search box on Facebook and looking for "prayers wanted" or similar terms. Then she'd look through the prayer requests for stories about kids with cancer, and she'd post about them to her fans. She asked her fans to go over to the other kids' pages (or their parents' pages) and post messages of encouragement. Soon she didn't need to search anymore—people would regularly write to her and ask, "Have you seen this page yet? This girl also has a brain tumor," or "Can you ask people to go Like this boy's fan page? He's starting treatment tomorrow."

She would post her call-out and then sit back and watch with excitement as the NEGU Nation swarmed the pages with positive messages. When I got back from work, it was often the first thing she wanted to tell me about.

"Daddy, we got four hundred Likes for Christopher today!"

"That's great, honey! Who's Christopher?"

"He's seven, and he has leukemia. He lives in Maine."

"Wow, all the way on the other side of the country. Now he has the NEGU Nation on his side too."

She loved watching those numbers climb. It meant more

people were praying, and the more people who were praying, the more likely it was for God to intervene. Aside from that, it was also just plain nice for families to feel that kind of support from compassionate strangers all around the world.

We came to call these requests "Joy Mobs." When Jessie saw someone in need, she would ask for a Joy Mob to go spread hope. The messages were often similar: "The Smith family is thinking of you today" or "Praying for you in Texas"—along with the word "NEGU."

The acronym NEGU took off quickly, with many people asking us how it was supposed to be pronounced. Jessie told them it was "knee-goo." What was cool for all of us was that it began popping up in places other than Facebook and among people we didn't know personally. It was even defined on an Internet slang website, showing it had crossed into popular usage.

People didn't know how bad things had gotten in our home. They didn't know that by the middle of radiation treatments, Jessie could no longer reliably stand by herself because of dizziness and weakness, so I had to carry her into the bathroom and hold her up in the shower while her mom stood outside the tub and washed her and shampooed her hair. They didn't know we had to cup our hands over her eyes because she couldn't close them and shampoo would sting them otherwise. They didn't hear her wailing in the middle of the night because her legs were cramping.

But they also didn't see her face light up because of the smallest kindnesses—birthday wishes, contributions to the JoyJars, and notes from people telling Jessie she had inspired them that day.

Of course, she wasn't just inspiring them. She was inspiring me too. If my daughter at eleven years old could manage to see a bigger picture during her battle with cancer, what could the rest of us accomplish? It felt like the best kind of challenge. It encouraged me and everyone else who encountered her to look inward and ask ourselves, "What have I done to make the world a better place today?"

How about you?

choke

Remember how I said Jessie hated needles? Well, when you have cancer, you have to face an extraordinary number of needles. Second only to the fear of the claustrophobic mask was the fear of having to get blood drawn at a minimum of once a week — every Thursday. They had to keep a close eye on her counts to make sure she could withstand treatments each week. Children can and do die from the treatments.

The first time she got her blood drawn, she met a phlebotomist named Jaime Serna. He was a charming man with a warm smile and quick sense of humor. Not only was he an expert at managing to make injections painless, but he was also an expert at putting kids at ease.

"Check this out!" he told her, inflating a balloon. Then he stuck a two-foot pin through the balloon without popping it. Jessie's eyes went wide.

The man used magic tricks to entertain the kids while they were having their blood drawn. He had a coloring book with all black-and-white drawings, but when a child tapped it with a magic wand, the pages would magically turn colors. He could make quarters disappear and reappear or turn water into confetti. It was quite a show.

He was a good-looking bodybuilder type, originally from Mexico City. In his time away from the hospital, he played a Power Rangers character on a local Hispanic television station. Jessie thought that was hilarious, and JT thought he was really cool.

When he was finished drawing her blood, Jessie looked at him with amazement and said, "That didn't even hurt!"

"Told you," he said. "If you ever need me, here is my pager number ..."

He wrote down his number for us and told Jessie that whenever she needed to have her blood drawn, she could call on him. If she wasn't able to come down to his lab, then he'd come to her wherever she was. She came to call him her personal vampire.

One massive anxiety lifted straight off all of our shoulders. If ever there was a person tailor-made for that job, Jaime was it. There are some people so kindhearted that you can just feel the love radiating out of them, and that was him. He loved every child who crossed his path.

So each Thursday, we'd insist on seeing only Jaime, and when she needed blood drawn in the clinic, the nurses would happily page him. He was divorced, and I suspect they enjoyed having him around just as much as Jessie did.

As I thought about the idea of enriching other people's lives and doing good in this world, Jaime became a shining example. He didn't need to show up at work with a red clown nose or a bag of magic tricks. That was nowhere in his job description. He didn't need to buy presents for his patients with money from his paycheck or organize special events for kids in the lobby. But his heart was bigger than his job title.

"I want them to come and see a friend, not a phlebotomist," he said.

I thought about a world filled with Jaimes and how amazing that would be. Imagine if each of us put as much love into our interactions with people as he does. Imagine if each of us went about our lives trying to figure out how to make someone else's day better. How would the world look different?

Stacey and I have taught our kids about empathy organically, not in any organized fashion. When things come up, we discuss them, and one topic that often came up in our household was people in need.

In addition to praying for people in our community who had health problems or were going through other crises, we also participated in several church outreach programs each year, such as Project Backpack (gathering school supplies for kids in need) and Operation Christmas Child, a project sponsored by Samaritan's Purse to deliver shoeboxes filled with toys to kids living in poverty all over the world during the Christmas season.

Each of our kids got to fill their own shoebox, and we didn't give them any monetary limit. We'd go out shopping together and see just how much we could stuff into our shoeboxes. Jessie in particular loved doing it every year. She had a superorganized mind and loved figuring out the logistics—*If I turn this little doll sideways, then I can fit another bracelet next to it.*

In some ways, those shoeboxes were a predecessor to JoyJars. Same concept, but for a different purpose.

Jessie felt so connected to Jaime in part because they were the same kind of people. She cared deeply about others and wanted to make people feel comfortable and connected. She was the kind of kid who wouldn't invite just some of the kids from her class to her birthday party; she wanted to invite the whole class so no one felt left out.

When a new girl named Carly joined the swim team, some of the other girls were playing a game that Carly didn't understand. Jessie tried to get the girls to include Carly, but when they didn't, Jessie simply stopped playing with them so this new girl wouldn't feel alone. They became close friends on that day. That's what empathy is all about—just taking simple actions to help make someone's life a little better.

It made me feel so good to hear that story, because I knew it meant Jessie understood what God asks of us. Sometimes on the ride home after the kids' church programs, we'd talk about the lessons they'd learned that day and I'd ask them to apply those lessons to our lives.

"So you learned that the Bible talks about the good Samaritan," I'd say. "What does that mean? How can we be good Samaritans?"

Stacey and I have always felt it's important to talk to our children like this so we can help them foster a sense of caring for those in need. Their views can otherwise become myopic. If they and their friends don't have to worry about where their next meal is coming from, how will they understand it's not like that for everyone? We have to tell them about the need and empower them to find ways to help.

Jessie was doing it through her JoyJars, but she was far from being the only young kid making a difference in this world. Take Hannah Turner, a girl who was just four years old when she helped her mother and siblings serve dinner on Thanksgiving Day to people in need at a church in Ohio in 2004. At one point, she noticed a man whose shoes were split open, revealing that he had no socks on. She tugged on her mom's sweater and said, "Mommy, won't his feet be cold?"

Despite her mom's reassurance that his shoes would keep his

feet warm enough, Hannah began removing her shoes and said, "Mommy, he can have my socks."

It was that expression of compassion that made this mom follow up on her daughter's wish. The next day, they went out and bought one hundred pairs of socks and donated them to the mission shelter. And that was almost that—except that the next Thanksgiving Day, the same man was back, and once again, Hannah tugged on her mother's sweater and said, "Mommy, I think he needs some more socks."

Ever since that day, they have been collecting new socks to give to shelters in their area. They learned that socks and undergarments were very rarely given to shelters but were badly needed, and so they began the charity, Hannah's Socks. They have collected socks from individuals and groups all over the country and even internationally, and they've also sponsored many events to raise money to buy socks. They've now given away hundreds of thousands of pairs of socks to shelters, and Hannah, now a teenager, remains the driving influence behind the charity.

Craig Kielburger was just twelve when he happened upon an article about a Pakistani boy who was also twelve when he was murdered for speaking out against child slave labor. The boy, Iqbal Masih, had been a slave himself. His parents sold him into slavery when he was four years old, and he had worked fourteen-hour days, seven days a week, at a carpet-weaving loom, where he was typically shackled. He escaped twice, and on the second escape, he joined a group called the Bonded Labour Liberation Front, an organization that aims to end child labor. He had been giving speeches around the world and had just returned from America when someone shot and killed him on Easter Sunday in 1995.

The article bothered Craig so much that he went to his class-mates and said, "Here is the problem—who wants to help?"

Eleven of them answered his call, and they met in his parents' living room to come up with a plan for the group, which they named Free the Children. These were not kids with great worldly knowledge, but they saw an injustice and decided to do something about it.

When *60 Minutes* reporter Ed Bradley asked Craig, "Why you?" Craig answered, "Why not? If everyone in the world could say, 'Why me?' then nothing would ever be accomplished."

Free the Children now has two million volunteers in forty-five countries, and most of the volunteers are children themselves. They work to help kids in Africa, Asia, and Latin America escape from poverty. They've built more than 650 schools or schoolrooms and sent more than sixteen million dollars' worth of medical supplies through their "Adopt a Village" program.

That's astounding, but there are also smaller-scale successes, like when seven-year-old Jack Henderson began selling his drawings to raise money for the hospital that took care of his little brother. Or every time a child volunteers at a nursing home, has a lemonade stand for charity, or helps a neighbor with a chore. The grand-scale efforts are wonderful, but so are the everyday acts of kindness.

I believe if we take the time to listen to our hearts about the things that bother us in the world and make the decision to do something rather than just feel bad about it, we can make life so much better for others and for ourselves.

Things were heating up with the NEGU movement quickly, and Rick Brotherton pointed out to us that Jessie's website, where she posted her blog updates, had already received 44,000 visitors from seventy-six countries. People started sending us pictures of the word "NEGU" showing up in unexpected places

—on a sign held by a soldier in the Middle East, written in the sand at the beach, etched in marker on someone's hand ... sometimes just the word, and other times a message like "We NEGU for Jessie." Jessie's sixth-grade classmates made her a big quilt with the letters NEGU written on blocks of fabric.

All of that encouraged her on days that were otherwise very discouraging—like the days when she just got tired of all the medications and their side effects. In mid-April, she began losing a little bit of hair from the chemotherapy and had some stomach upset. She dealt with the dizziness and varying muscle weakness and cramping, the facial swelling, the insomnia—all of it—but the one thing that bothered her more than anything else was the difficulty she had with swallowing.

That came to a head one night at the dinner table. It was a night no one in the family has ever been able to recover from completely, and it's an image I think will always be burned into my memory as a terrible turning point.

Like every other night, we were eating together, sitting in our regular spots. Then Jessie choked on a French fry. Expecting it to clear quickly, I just looked at her and waited a second, but then she gave me a look that said, *I'm scared.* She was really choking. She couldn't breathe, and her face registered panic.

I pushed my chair out of the way to make a beeline around the table to Jessie, nearly knocking over two of our dogs in the process. I stood her up, grabbed her in the Heimlich maneuver position, and thrust my hands just under her rib cage to force out the food she was choking on. It was terrifying. I had never done the Heimlich maneuver, and I was sure I wasn't doing it correctly, but thank goodness, it worked on the first try. The food came out, and Jessie started crying in a mix of fear and embarrassment. The whole episode had probably lasted just thirty seconds, but as all traumas do, it seemed to go on much longer.

"I hate this!" Jessie said.

I looked up after the crisis was over and realized my other two children were missing. They had both fled the room during the commotion. Stacey and I got Jessie calmed down and then went looking for the others. We found Shaya crying in the hallway.

"What's wrong?" I asked.

"I'm scared," she said.

"Your sister is okay. It's over. She's not choking anymore. Do you know where JT is?"

"Yes, he's in your office."

I found him hiding under my desk, as if he were sheltering himself from an earthquake.

"Hey, buddy," I said, trying to sound casual. "What's going on?"

"That really scared me, Daddy," he said.

For all the reassurances we had given them about the brain tumor, the kids hadn't really been scared until that moment. The choking episode was what made it real for them. This was serious, and their sister was in danger.

It had a devastating impact on Jessie too. She became afraid to eat. She had already lost five pounds up to that point, so she could not only not afford to lose more weight but also needed to keep eating to keep up her strength for continued treatments. We begged her to try, but she acted as if food were her enemy.

That was as scary to me as the tumor itself. Imagine going through all this, only to have her pass away not from cancer but from not eating?

"Please, just take a little bite," I'd say. Stacey tried tempting her with all her favorite foods, but for a long while, nothing worked.

Even weeks later, when we were sure she could physically swallow again, it remained an emotional hurdle. Her doctor took X-rays and did tests of her gag reflex to show that the swelling had gone down and there was no reason for her concern. Her gag reflex was working fine and she wouldn't be unable to breathe if she choked — but it had no effect. Jessie still wouldn't eat.

Adding to the problem was the fact that her steroid, Decadron, was in pill form and she refused to swallow it. Stacey would cut it, crush it up, and put it in yogurt, and it was still a battle to get her to take it. She'd take the tiniest bit of yogurt, and we'd have to argue with her to finish it. Just a couple of spoonfuls of yogurt — just enough for one little pill. It was worrisome, and the doctor threatened to put a scope down her throat to show her she could physically swallow.

"You have to try harder," she told Jessie. "You won't get well if you aren't taking your medicine and eating properly."

We added it to our prayer requests. We would pray with the kids by their bedsides every night, and they would always ask God to "please heal Jessie's tumor," adding requests about any specific symptoms that were troubling her — like, "Please help Jessie walk." Now our prayers always included, "Please help Jessie eat."

I knew how strong her fear was because it reminded me of a time a couple of years earlier when she was trying to qualify for the Junior Olympics in the butterfly stroke. She was halfway across the pool when she inhaled some water and started choking. She came to a complete halt in the middle of the pool.

"You're okay. Keep going!" we called out to her, and she finished the race. The next couple of months of swimming were difficult for her because she couldn't get the thought of choking out of her mind. Now it was the same feeling, only it was connected to something far worse.

There were still moments of happiness in the midst of our troubles. Jessie was so focused on helping others, but I was focused on helping Jessie. Don't get me wrong—I loved doing the JoyJars and seeing how they helped other kids, but I loved it first because Jessie loved it. Anything I could do to brighten her day was worth trying.

What that meant to me was that I called in every favor I could.

Stacey and I have not been financially rich, but we have been "people rich." We've been very blessed to have strong relationships with truly caring people who have stepped up to help every time we've needed it.

One of Jessie's favorite things to do with her family was watch *American Idol*, so I put out the word to ask if anyone could help us get tickets. I had hoped we could get two tickets so Stacey or I could take Jessie—even better if we could get five tickets so the whole family could go together. We got ten.

Friends of ours approached executive producer Ron DeShay, who asked staff members to give up their tickets for us so Jessie would have prime seating. We were able to take not only our whole family but also Mrs. Moore (one of Jessie's favorite teachers); one of Shaya's best friends, Katie, and her mom, Mary; and Rick Brotherton and his daughter, Casey. We thought it was a nice way to thank Rick for all he'd done to put his life on hold to help us get the JoyJars project under way.

Jessie was rooting for Casey Abrams, the quirky, redheaded jazz musician who lived in Southern California, so Rick designed a professional sign for Jessie to hold up that said "NEGU Casey."

Then my best friend Jeff's family hired a limousine to take

us to the show. Once we got there, we were in for an even bigger surprise: We had VIP status—which meant, among other things, that we got to use a special entrance and meet Randy Jackson in the greenroom before the show.

Jessie was wearing her pink glitter Toms shoes, and Randy was wearing crazy glitter boots. It was the perfect conversation starter.

"Hey, nice shoes!" Randy said. "We almost match. What do you think of mine?"

"They're great," Jessie said with a giggle. She was wearing her face mask and was self-conscious at first, but he put her at ease. He was very gracious and kind, making light conversation and taking pictures with us. Soon it was time to get to our seats. The adults were split up, but all the kids and Stacey got to sit up front together.

Just when we thought the day couldn't get better, Ryan Seacrest came over during a commercial break and asked Jessie if she'd like to introduce the next singer—eventual winner Scotty McCreary. Everyone watching from home got to see Jessie on TV! They showed her again when another finalist, Jacob Lusk, stood next to her and waved from the audience. Her Facebook page exploded with friends writing, "I saw you on television. You looked beautiful!"

After the idols performed, the crew cleared the stage and set it up again for a mini Katy Perry concert. Katy came out and performed three songs that would be shown on the following night's show.

"We're so lucky!" Jessie said. "Can you believe it?"

We got to go backstage afterward, and the singers were very friendly to us and posed for lots of pictures and signed autographs for the kids. Jessie showed Casey her sign and gave him a NEGU bracelet, which he wore on two upcoming shows. He even pointed to it and mouthed "Never ever give up" at the end of one episode. Jessie wore her mask for much of the day, but we didn't have the heart to make her wear it for all her special memory moments. She took it off while she was being shown on camera and for some of the meet-and-greet pictures.

"They're all so pretty!" Jessie exclaimed about the women, who were perfectly made up and styled.

There were several other visitors with VIP passes that day, including a boy with a Make-A-Wish button. His wish had been to come to this show.

Jessie beamed that day—the whole day. It was awesome to see my little fighter with her spirits up, moving around fairly well and so energized to meet the people behind one of her favorite television shows. I wished her life could be like this every day—nothing but joy—making her forget for a little while the realities of her life. *I* wanted to forget the realities of her life too. I watched her run her fingers across her VIP necklace and thought about how much I wanted the world to know that this was a very important person—a special girl who didn't deserve to suffer.

A girl who didn't deserve to die.

The high we all got from the *American Idol* experience made me seek out more adventures. I wondered what else I could do to surprise and encourage her, so I began writing to some of her favorite celebrities by e-mail and on Twitter, asking them to make a little video of themselves saying, "We NEGU ... do you?"

What was the worst that could happen? I'd get ignored, or someone might say no. That didn't concern me. The best that could happen was seeing that I could help Jessie through this awful time—and that was worth a million noes.

I had not been active on social media before Jessie's diagnosis, but now I learned as much as I could. A friend of mine who's active on Twitter started campaigns enlisting others to ask singer Carrie Underwood and TV host Jeff Probst from *Survivor* to make videos for Jessie, and they both did. Both times, I'd received word they were going to do it, but I still pretended to have no idea what was going on when the videos came in.

"Hmm, I just got this e-mail. Let's see what this is. Oh, look —it's a video!" I'd say to Jessie, and she'd squeal with glee.

One of the coolest things about Jessie was her inability to hide her emotions. She would laugh the hardest and cry the hardest of anyone in the family. Every holiday was more special because of Jessie's heightened sense of anticipation. Even when she was a toddler, she would burst with joy every time someone's birthday or other special occasion was on the horizon. Simple things made her so happy, like when Tanta and her great-uncle Bob made her a treasure chest for Christmas with See's Candies gold coins inside when she was three or four years old, and she threw the coins in the air and laughed with such excitement. Jessie's belly laugh was contagious, and she felt things so deeply, both positive and negative. These NEGU videos were definitely positives. Whenever a new one came in, it made her day and mine.

They weren't just from celebrities, but from people all over the world. Some were messages directly for Jessie, and some were general "Never Ever Give Up" messages for all the kids fighting cancer.

Someone—and I still have no idea who—even blew me away with a great surprise. I don't know how they found out about us, but two ESPN SportsCenter anchors sent a picture. That was the most exciting one for me. I've been a sports nut forever, and these were guys I've watched and admired for years. To see them holding a sign that read "We NEGU ... do you?" gave me the biggest boost. So many people who seemed very important had taken time out of their lives to join in this movement started by an eleven-year-old girl. It was beautiful.

Those were the highs I tried to carry in my heart to get us through the lows. One of the most difficult side effects for us was just getting started—mood changes resulting from the steroids.

Jessie was on high doses of steroids, and when she started having bad days, I tried hard to keep in mind what people had told me about giving kids on steroids a "wide berth." Suddenly, my always-sweet daughter was rolling her eyes and snapping at us, turning her head and saying, "Whatever!" when her mom or Nana asked her to do something, usually having to do with taking medication or eating.

Nana didn't let her get away with it. She wanted to treat Jessie like the other two kids. JT noticed it too, because Jessie was acting bossy and annoyed when he sat with her to do homework. Stacey, on the other hand, just took it and accepted that Jessie wasn't herself.

Whenever Jessie realized she'd been out of line, she'd apologize afterward. Twice, I can remember her crying about it.

"I know I'm being edgy, but I can't stop myself," she said. "I don't feel like me."

"It's just the medication you're on. This won't last much longer. Just do the best you can," Stacey reassured her.

We didn't take it to heart when she got snappy, but it was hard to see her lose control of her moods. So much of it had to do with the choking episode. She did not want to eat at all, and while we catered to her in the beginning and served up lots of smoothies and shakes—things she wouldn't have to chew and wasn't afraid she would choke on—we knew she needed more than that. She needed calories. She couldn't go through such intensive cancer treatments with so little nutrition, but the thought of food threw her into a panic.

Kimmy and T were flying in from Denver as often as they could during this time, usually taking turns. One of them was with us nearly every weekend, and T noticed that Jessie wouldn't snap at him, so he helped as much as he could. Sometimes he would take Jessie to the movies to give her a change of scenery, since she was now spending an awful lot of time at home. Going to the movies wasn't strenuous. She could just sit in the audience and wear her face mask in the dark theater.

They did whatever they could to get her to smile. One of the things that still cracked her up pretty regularly was "Bean-Boozling" people. BeanBoozled is a type of Jelly Belly jelly bean that has ten regular flavors and ten disgusting ones. You can't tell which is which because each "good" flavor has a gross one in a matching color—so you might be getting banana or pencil shavings, caramel corn or moldy cheese. She loved foisting these on people and laughing her head off when they made faces about the terrible flavors. Mommy and Daddy were pretty good sports about it, but it was also a rite of passage among our visitors. Chances are that if you came to our house during this period, you were going to get BeanBoozled.

"Ugh, what was that?" was a pretty common refrain.

"Rotten egg!" Jessie would say as she practically rolled off the couch in a fit of laughter.

T accompanied us to a radiation treatment one day and was amazed at how casually Jessie had come to take it. They sat together in the waiting room, and the technician called her in. By then, the calls of "Jessica Rees?" had turned into "Jessie."

"It's time," the man said.

Jessie took off the big yellow scarf she was wearing and wrapped it around T's neck, giving him a big hug. I took a picture of them like that. Then she took the technician's hand and walked away.

While she was gone, T got to feel exactly what we had gone through all those weeks — the helplessness, knowing she was strapped down in the next room all alone.

"I don't know how you do this every day," he said.

"Me neither."

"This really sucks."

It took me aback for a moment. He had skipped right past all the platitudes that people usually lean on — all the words of comfort you say when you really don't know what else to say. For two months, I was used to hearing, "God has a plan," and "Hang in there," and "I'm sure she'll get through this" — and those were the same sorts of things I was saying too. But it was also amazing to finally hear someone tell it like it was.

Because it did suck.

It sucked that my daughter could barely walk anymore. It sucked that she was now salivating so much that she carried a spit cup wherever she went. It sucked that she felt so lonely and limited. It sucked that she was terrified to eat and that my other kids had been traumatized to watch her choke. It sucked that my Jessie had brain cancer. It all just sucked!

On this day, like every other day, I tried so hard to make sense of things through prayer. I focused on one of Jessie's favorite verses, Joshua 1:9: "Be strong and courageous. Do not be afraid; do not be discouraged, for the LORD your God will be with you wherever you go." She claimed that as the core verse for TeamNEGU because of all the courageous kids fighting cancer.

She lived that verse. I tried to be as courageous as she was. I prayed for strength for all of us. I prayed for courage. And I prayed for the miracle. *Please, God, heal my daughter.*

We adults sat there comforting each other, getting through the longest ten minutes of the day, until she emerged again.

"Only three songs!" she said with a big smile.

That's how our lives would be measured—not in misery, but in song.

First day of 6th grade, with JT and Shaya

Jessie with Nana and Papa a few days after being diagnosed with cancer

Jessie enjoying a cupcake at a friend's birthday party, weeks prior to being diagnosed with cancer

Jessie hanging out with members of USA Swimming at the very first JoySplash fund-raiser

Jessie competing at a swim meet prior to diagnosis

JT, Jessie, and Shaya laughing at the beach a few days after Jessie was diagnosed on March 3, 2011

The Rees family poses for a special photo with Jessie a few days after being told she has cancer

Jessie hanging out in the greenroom with *American Idol* contestants

Jessie making the very first JoyJars for children fighting cancer in the hospital

Jessie showing off her radiation mask after completing her thirty rounds of treatment

Celebrating Jessie's twelfth birthday with a special two-layer custom cake

Jessie's best friend, Sophie, visits her at home and gives her a special blanket to stay cozy

Shaya, Jessie, and JT during their special weekend at Disneyland, celebrating the end of Jessie's first week of treatment

Jessie enjoying a special visit with two of her favorite teachers: Kim Moore (1st grade) and Debbie James (5th grade)

Jessie with her phlebotomist Jaime, preparing to get her blood drawn

Jessie and Mommy waiting to see the doctor at Children's Hospital of Orange County

Jessie being examined by her favorite doctor (Jody Pathare) during one of her countless visits to Children's Hospital of Orange County

Special cake for Jessie, celebrating the completion of her thirty rounds of radiation

Jessie standing by her giant wall of encouragement decorated with well-wishings from teammates, classmates, and friends

Jessie displaying her 6th grade project titled Foodopia — the island of goodies

Jessie with the prizes her amazing teammates won for her during the Clovis swim meet trip

Jessie with her daddy, Erik, moments after being baptized by him in their Jacuzzi

Jessie with CBS 2 News reporter Lisa Sigell, hanging out at home playing with JoyJars after the video shoot was over

Jessie shaving her daddy's head as he goes bald for brain tumor awareness

Pastor Buddy Owens leading a special prayer time for Jessie during the "night of worship" at Saddleback Church

Jessie donating $500 to members of her care team at Children's Hospital of Orange County to help find a cure for cancer

Jessie hanging out with her teammates during a Mission Viejo Nadadores swim meet

Jessie holding up her special NEGU sign to encourage the world to Never Ever Give Up!

Jessie hanging out with Uncle T after they went swimming with dolphins

Jessie holding her new puppy, Moe, the day he arrived from Texas

Jessie with Aunt Kimmy at the first NEGU Golf Classic

Summer vacation at Kukio in Kona with JT, Mommy, Jessie, Daddy, and Shaya

JT and Jessie showing off their new leis from Aunt Kimmy after arriving in Kona to start their special vacation

Jessie enjoying the "swimming with dolphins" experience in Kona during summer vacation

Jessie enjoying the warm waters in Kukio Bay during summer vacation in Kona

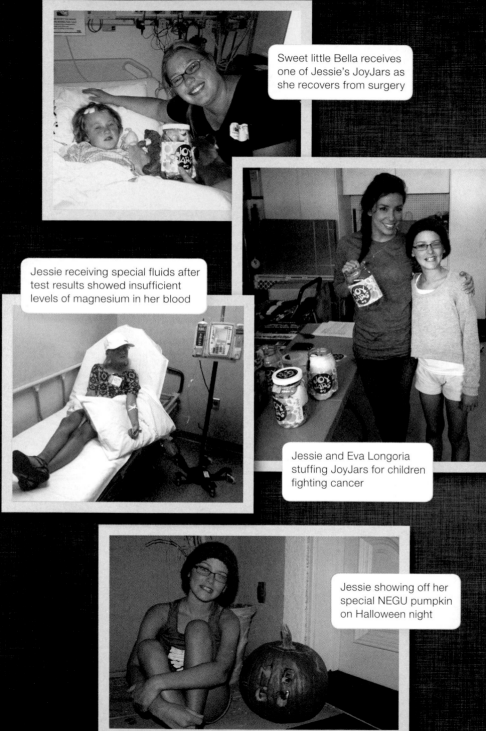

Sweet little Bella receives one of Jessie's JoyJars as she recovers from surgery

Jessie receiving special fluids after test results showed insufficient levels of magnesium in her blood

Jessie and Eva Longoria stuffing JoyJars for children fighting cancer

Jessie showing off her special NEGU pumpkin on Halloween night

Jessie with her swim coach Bryan Dedeaux at the finish line of his triathlon, which he dedicated to her. She and Coach Bryan had a very special bond.

Jessie watching TV during a chemo treatment at Children's Hospital of Orange County

Jessie standing outside with 2,000 empty jars to be used for her JoyJars. Jessie stuffed and sent more than 3,000 JoyJars during her fight against cancer.

Jessie at City of Hope Hospital, getting ready to deliver JoyJars to children fighting cancer

Jessie visiting sweet little Bella after finishing their chemotherapy treatment at Children's Hospital of Orange County

Jessie, Shaya, and Erik enjoying a special time with Eva Longoria and Marcia Cross on the set of *Desperate Housewives* in Hollywood

Jessie with Aunt Kimmy, showing off their gingerbread house during Christmas vacation in Denver

Master artist Tom Clark showcases his special JOY painting created during Jessie's Celebration of Life service. The painting now hangs in the Rees home.

More than 5,000 people attended Jessie's Celebration of Life service at Saddleback Church

Friends decorated an overpass fence with Jessie's NEGU motto just a few days after she lost her fight against cancer

Thousands mourn icon of pediatric cancer

Jessica Joy Rees, 12, inspired others with her motto: 'Never Ever Give Up.'

By LORI BASHEDA and ERIKA I. RITCHIE
THE ORANGE COUNTY REGISTER

LAKE FOREST • More than 3,400 people flocked to Saddleback Church on Wednesday night to remember the life of seventh-grader Jessica Joy Rees with tears, song and praise.

It was an emotional service, led by the 12-year-old girl's father, Erik Rees, a pastor at Saddleback, and

COURT
Erik Rees comforts Sophia Spad
ca's best friend, who had writte
miracle. When she left us, we r
cle." Sophia sobbed beside hi

AN EDITION OF REGISTER

RANCHO SANTA I
NEWS

Jessica Joy Rees takes a photo with her parents, Stacey and Erik Rees. Jessie and her family have built a community of support
as she battles an inoperable brain tumor, with more than 13,000 followers on her Facebook page. | PHOTO COURTESY OF REES FAMILY

JESSIE'S JOY JARS

RANCHO GIRL, 12, HELPS OTHERS BY RAISING MONEY FOR LIFE-THREATENING PEDIATRIC ILLNESSES.   PAGE 6

t her sp
Even as the la
radiation limited her au
to mo
uld sm
uld."
He
anks
"g
r a
f.
d

South County

Patient seeks to spread joy

RANCHO SANTA MARGARITA • Friends and family use the words thoughtful, fun, silly and caring in describing Jessica Rees.

Most call her by her nickname "Jessie," but it's her middle name that might describe her best: Joy.

KRISTY CHU
REGISTER WRITER

Jessica Joy Rees, 12, is on a mission to spread joy to others through a creation she calls JoyJars. The idea is simple: purchase a

PHOTOS: COURTESY OF THE REES FAMILY
emotherapy.

WEDNESDAY 11PM NEWS

It was in her visits to
CHOC that Jessie came up

stay strong.
Find out more at
jessiejoyrees.com

A box containing JoyJars.

---

http://www.yahoo.com/
craigslist   HootSuite   Bible   ESV Online   Google Voice   Albms   WHOIS   POSTIN

YAHOO!®
Web   Images   Video   Local   Apps   M

Saturday, January 7, 2012

YAHOO! SITES
- Mail
- Autos
- Dating
- Finance (Dow $)
- Flickr
- Games
- Horoscopes
- Jobs
- Messenger

Young cancer victim loses public battle
Jessica Joy Rees, just 12, gained national recognition while blogging about her fight.
'Never ever give up.'
• Cannon: 'Good prognosis'
• Cancer rates falling

Girl, 12, Is Called An Inspiration As She Battles Devastating Illness

Jessie Rees
DAUGHTER

CBS
2

Dow Nasdaq
PARTNERS

A collection of pictures and news clippings showcasing Jessie and her JoyJars

exposed

There are risks to putting your whole life on the Internet, and I don't just mean safety risks. There are emotional risks inherent in exposing your thoughts and feelings to thousands of strangers.

When we started up Jessie's blog and posts, at first, it was entirely positive. Kids who wouldn't have otherwise known Jessie began writing to her. Friends kept in touch through messaging, even though she was no longer in school or at swimming practice with them.

But there did come a day when I got a text at work from T.

"Did you see that guy's nasty comment on Jessie's page?"

I quickly clicked on the page to check it out, and sure enough, someone had left a terrible comment after Jessie posted a thank-you to all of the people who had sent her gifts and cards. "You're using your cancer to try to get presents for yourself!" he wrote.

He had, of course, received a pretty massive smackdown from Jessie's fans, but his comment was still there, and by the time I deleted it, several family members had already seen it. I found out this is a common occurrence on pages devoted to people with health crises. Some lousy person somewhere will manage to twist it into a "scheme." Sure, Jessie was going through inoperable brain cancer *just to get presents*.

Absurd things like this should never ruin one's day, and yet I can't pretend it didn't. That one guy brought a few more crazies out of the woodwork. Some of our family members left heated responses, and before long, I found myself deleting comments and banning people several times that day.

"If they knew us at all, they'd never say these things," I told myself. But maybe they would. Some people refuse to see honesty and pure intentions. For them, life is all about cynicism and conspiracies. These are the people for whom the phrase "No good deed goes unpunished" was coined.

Stacey and I had to tell Jessie what was going on because we felt the need to create a written response to it. She cried at the thought that someone would think so badly of her.

"Honey, what you're doing is a great thing. These people are not being kind. They're not worth your energy," I said, and then I wrote a statement telling people that this was not acceptable on Jessie's page.

"If you have any concerns, feel free to write to me," I wrote. "This is not the place to express your negative opinions about Jessie or her JoyJars."

It didn't stop the rude comments permanently, but at least they slowed down for a while. Even now, I occasionally have to delete and block people who look for ways to cut us down.

Of course, there have been true stories about corrupt charities or people faking illnesses in order to get donations. We were even duped once ourselves. One of the pages Jessie had Liked on Facebook about a woman whose child had cancer turned out to be a hoax. It amazes me that anyone could sink so low as to prey on people's sympathy in that way. But it also amazes me that anyone could paint all the rest of us with that same brush when it's clear that most people *aren't* pulling a hoax. Picking on a child with cancer on a page dedicated to her healing takes a special kind of jerk.

When a movement begins to garner greater attention, there is a tendency to run into more of those people, which is what was happening with us. Jessie's fan page had a lot of Likes and activity—which in itself bothered some people who were also trying to raise awareness of pediatric cancer. A new friend whose daughter also had DIPG admitted to me once over lunch that he felt angry because Jessie was getting so much attention for her JoyJars and his daughter didn't have any sort of "thing" going, so he felt like she couldn't compete.

"Please don't compare," I told him. "We're all in this together."

It really wasn't about who had more Facebook Likes, but about his struggles with feeling that the fight was pointless. At least having a community of supporters surrounding you can give more fuel to keep you going. When I got home that day, I asked Jessie's supporters to Joy Mob his daughter's page—which he loved. Encouragement means so much when you have so little.

If I had thought about how Jessie's JoyJars project was doing in comparison, say, to Alex's Lemonade Stand, then I might have felt really bad. Alex's project has raised more than $60 million for pediatric cancer research and become a nationally recognized name, with big banner advertising in places like Toys"R"Us. But it's also been around since 2000, and our journey was just beginning.

When it became clear that we were going to go beyond just our local hospital with the JoyJars, we began talking about setting up a nonprofit foundation.

"Let's call it the Jessica Rees Foundation," I said.

"No, I don't want my name used," she said.

"What do you want to call it?"

"How about the NEGU Foundation?"

That's what we did. Together with Kimmy and an attorney friend of hers who worked pro bono, we filled out all the paperwork, making decisions about what type of nonprofit we wanted to have and what our goals would be.

"Do you want it to be about cure or care?" I asked. There were different categories, depending on whether we wanted to focus on cancer research or patient care.

"Care," she said.

I could have guessed she'd say that. Cancer research is vital, but so is care, especially when someone is dealing with a cancer like DIPG with such a dismal prognosis. She didn't understand the science behind the medical interventions, but she did understand the idea of bringing comfort to kids in treatment.

Our initial mission statement was "to spread hope and joy to children and families affected by life-threatening pediatric medical conditions, encouraging them to Never Ever Give Up by staying emotionally and physically strong!" It was a bit cumbersome, but it fit the bill.

We began planning our first major fund-raiser, a golf tournament to be held in September—National Pediatric Cancer Awareness Month. Knowing it could take six months to get our nonprofit status approved, we filed an expedited application. We were approved in ten days, which is unheard-of.

We got our nonprofit status shortly after Jessie's last radiation treatment on April 29. It was an important landmark for us —no more daily trips to CHOC, no more radiation mask, the side effects of the radiation would slowly wear off. They couldn't stop the steroids all at once, though. The weaning process would be very slow, lasting all the way into June. And she still had forty-eight days of oral chemotherapy left before the next phase of her treatment would begin, plus weekly check-ins for her blood work and various therapies and tests of her progress.

The first MRI after her radiation caused a roller coaster of emotion. It was the first opportunity to find out if the treatments were working, and it was terrifying to wait for a page of results that held the analysis of my daughter's future. I knew not to expect the tumor to be gone; the best we could realistically hope for was a reduction in size. The other possible outcomes were for it to stay the same or for it to continue growing, having been unresponsive to the treatment.

Although I tried hard to convey that this was going to be a long treatment and that we shouldn't expect too much so soon, of course Jessie got her hopes up anyway.

"I hope they tell me the tumor is gone," she wrote the night before the MRI. "I don't want to think about this tumor anymore."

Of course, that was my hope too. We prayed the doctor's report would read "NED"—no evidence of disease—but I couldn't let my heart grab hold of that. Daily, I tried to keep my head out of the clouds and remind myself of the realities of what we were up against.

The results came by e-mail, written in medical language so thick that no one without a medical degree could make heads or tails of it. Luckily, the doctor had written a helpful translation on top: the tumor had shrunk by almost 30 percent.

It was a good day.

"We'll do another MRI in three months and see how the tumor has responded then," the doctor said.

"Wait ... three months? Why would you wait that long?"

"That's what the insurance requires."

"That's crazy. The tumor could be growing for three months before we'd ever even know. No, I want to know when that train is coming. I want as much notice as I can have if it starts to grow again."

"It's not our decision, unfortunately."

"Then I'll take it up with the insurance company."

And I did. After several calls, I received approval to have Jessie's MRIs done every month instead of every three months. Of course, that wasn't Jessie's favorite thing to have done. The MRIs were done in a building across from CHOC, where she couldn't have Jaime do her injections. And these had to be done with contrast dye, which was more painful than a regular injection. She hated getting the contrast dye, and depending on the expertise of the injector or the luck of where it landed that day, it ranged from being uncomfortable to being awful.

That was another item added to our prayer list every month: "Please let the contrast dye go in painlessly."

As soon as we got the MRI results, I told Jessie to post them online so people would know there had been an improvement. She got lots of congratulations and cheers, and it took several days before a couple of people in our family worked up the nerve to call us and say, "Hey, we don't want to find out about this stuff on Facebook. Don't you think you could call us first?"

They were 100 percent right, and I asked for forgiveness. From then on, we sent texts to family members before any big announcements went online. It was another lesson for me about how to conduct ourselves online, though not my last.

Weeks earlier, I had posted the photo of T wearing Jessie's big yellow scarf when he accompanied her to radiation, because I didn't know at the time that not everyone found Facebook as therapeutic as I did. To Jessie and me, these people—yes, mostly strangers—were a huge source of support. We let them in on many personal aspects of our lives because it felt right. I wanted them to know all they could about us so they'd know who they were praying for and why. T felt too exposed, though. He even started getting recognized around town when he flew in after that photo was posted.

"Hey, you're Uncle T!" someone said to him at the airport.

It was strange for him — nice because it showed him how deeply people were invested in Jessie's life, but also painful because he felt like people were watching the most difficult thing he'd ever gone through. It was like when the media shows up after a tragedy and starts interviewing people — only our tragedy was still in progress.

I didn't know, and he didn't tell me — at least not then. He knew we were too invested in our online world to squash that outlet for us. It was one of the earliest signs of the differences in personality types within our family and our ways of coping, though. For me, the more public, the better. It meant more prayers, more encouragement, and more help with Jessie's mission. Although I'm not an extrovert at heart, I pushed my boundaries because I believe there is something very powerful about having masses of people praying together.

That's why I called an old friend of mine, Lisa Sigell. I hadn't seen Lisa since high school, but I knew she was now an anchorperson at our local CBS affiliate and had a Health Watch segment. I wrote and told her about Jessie's mission and our newly minted NEGU Foundation.

"Jessie is giving out JoyJars to kids with cancer in local hospitals. Do you think you could do a story about her?"

Lisa was happy to set it up. She came to our home to interview us, and it was an all-day affair where we got to appreciate everything that goes into putting together a news segment. Lights are adjusted and readjusted; sound quality is sampled;

anything making a background noise is turned off or shooed out of the room. It took several hours to tape. Jessie was nervous beforehand because we didn't know what questions would be asked, but Lisa's warm personality put her at ease.

She first interviewed Stacey and me, asking questions about what it was like to be a pastor dealing with such a personal crisis.

"This is different from going and sitting with a family as a pastor, because I'm just Dad. My daughter doesn't need a pastor; she needs her daddy," I said.

Jessie sat alone on the couch for her interview. There were several questions about her treatments and then about JoyJars. Lisa asked, "Why are you doing this? Why not make it all about you?"

Jessie looked down for a moment and said, "Because that's not what it's about." Then she started to cry.

No one was expecting that, and I stood there for a moment before the cameraman signaled me to go ahead and comfort her. I put my arms around her, and Jessie just sobbed. She hadn't thought the emotion would come flowing out like that, and she was embarrassed about it afterward.

"Daddy, don't let them put that on television," she said to me. "I don't want everyone to see me crying."

I asked Lisa if they could leave out that part, but they couldn't. It was such a touching moment, and I understood why they wanted to show it. They did promise not to show too much of her crying. Not only did they not want to embarrass her, but they also wanted to make sure that the takeaway message was one of hope, not sadness.

It aired a few days later at 11:00 p.m., too late for the kids to stay up and watch, which was just as well. We got to preview it before they saw it and were happy with the tasteful job CBS did.

We knew it would mean more prayers for a miracle, more fans for Jessie's page, and more support for the JoyJars.

Jessie watched it with us the next day, but Shaya and JT decided not to. They knew Jessie had cried, and they didn't want to see their sister break down on television. What we were all going through was hard enough.

A bunch of kids in JT's class once started talking about Jessie and what they'd heard about her — "Hey, your sister has cancer!"

"Is she going to die?" one of them asked.

"No!" JT said, because he didn't know what else to say.

"That's what happens when you get cancer. You die."

"You do not!"

He had come home very upset that day. It wasn't that anyone meant to traumatize him; it's just that third graders have no filters. They say what they think without a lot of awareness of how their words are going to affect others. It was another example of the insensitivity that can arise when everybody knows your story.

And then even Stacey got hit. She doesn't like to write and isn't as Internet savvy or public about her feelings, so she didn't post on Facebook. Along with Jessie, I was the voice of the foundation, and several other family members would respond to our posts regularly. Finally, someone chirped up to ask, "Why isn't Jessie's mother ever on here? Doesn't she care?"

That flattened Stacey for two days. And what I wanted to say but didn't was, *Doesn't she care? Do you have any idea what my wife does every day? We're talking about a triathlete, a competitive swimmer. Stacey hasn't exercised since the day of Jessie's diagnosis. She hasn't done a thing she used to care about. Nothing else matters to her besides this family. This is a mom who doesn't leave her daughter's side except to work. A mom who takes her to every appointment, reads with her, prays with her, cooks for her, cries with her, gets her dressed, helps her walk, stays up with her when she can't sleep, teaches her, comforts her, holds her hand, and never lets her see that Mom's heart is shattered all over the floor. She is Jessie's hero. This is a woman trying to make it through the day on faith alone, when her little girl is expected to die by the time she's thirteen — and you think you care more than she does because you posted "Get well soon" on Facebook?*

Despite those limited bad experiences, we never regretted making Jessie's story so public. I believe we as people are better together. I believe in the power of community — of reaching out to others and asking for help when we need it and giving help whenever we can. I believe that's what God calls us to do for each other, and that sharing a heavy burden with people makes that burden a lot lighter. Cancer was a great burden on us, but the great people who reached out at every opportunity strengthened us and kept our spirits from crashing.

It's something I've believed in since I was a child and began seeking friendships to make up for the lack of family in my life. I was determined to give my children the sense of family I never had. And so from the time they were born, we did all we could to involve our families in their daily lives. We didn't take vacations alone. All of our vacations were with extended family members. We made a point of visiting and calling, sending pictures, keeping people updated on our lives, and staying on top of what was happening in theirs.

I didn't know what it meant to be a "family man" until I became one. And then it was an addictive feeling, wanting to build on to our kids' sense of family by drawing close friends into our circle. It was never a matter of needing popularity but of knowing our neighbors and church members for the betterment of all of us. When someone is in need, we can band together and help. I didn't expect to ever be the one "in need," but, then, there we were.

I've seen many people curl inward when going through something tragic. They're afraid to ask for help or to expose their vulnerabilities. They don't want to inconvenience people or whine or drag others down, or they don't want to be seen as weak. But there are so many people who want to help—people who love you, or would if you'd let them know you—who genuinely want to contribute when someone is in need. They just need a little direction.

That's why Jessie was very specific in her requests. Instead of just asking people to pray for her, she'd offer the specifics of what she needed help with that day, whether it was for a painless injection or an improved MRI. And when we started the foundation, I was specific in my requests too: Share our page with others so we can grow; buy a JoyJar to give to a friend and your purchase will enable us to send a JoyJar to a child with cancer; ask your Girl Scout troop or camp to sponsor a Joy Drive and fill boxes with new toys we can use to stuff our jars. All we had to do was ask, and people were happy to oblige. The more you can specify ways for people to get involved, the better your odds of getting what you need. And the more you share your gratitude with those who've helped, the better your odds of *continuing* to receive all the blessings they can share.

The Internet became an invaluable extension of our social circle. When Jessie didn't feel like "herself," she could still pull it together enough to go online and read. On any given day, there were dozens of messages waiting for her, each like a little burst of positive energy. "It helps a ton," she would say. My sweet pea loved people. And thanks to the Internet, many more people came to love Jessie.

mr. moe

You know how a child's first picture with Santa is usually a crying one? Well, imagine that sentiment when I tell you that one day in June, we had an unexpected visitor at CHOC. We were in the clinic for our weekly checkup and reported that, among other things, Jessie's leg cramping just wouldn't let up and we didn't know what to do for her. And she had lost hearing in her right ear because of the radiation. And she was still afraid to eat. Dr. Shen was there, along with a physician's assistant, a case manager, and a nurse, and Jessie was on the exam table.

She had just done a gag reflex test, one of her least favorite experiences in the world, but it's an important test because the tumor eventually impinges on a child's ability to gag. That's when eating really does become dangerous. I had already spoken with a parent whose child with DIPG passed away while choking on a muffin. The father had gone out for a quick run, and when he got back, he found his son in a chair, no longer breathing. What guilt that poor father lived with, as if he could have predicted anything like that happening.

As long as you're still gagging, you're okay, as unpleasant as it may be. Jessie was still gagging. So we were just coming down from that tension when a superenergetic and brightly attired blonde-haired woman bounded into the room.

"Jessie, I'm here to tell you you're getting a wish. I'm here to talk to you about your Make-A-Wish experience."

Now, Jessie didn't cry, but she did stiffen up considerably. All eyes were on her, expecting her to break into a big smile, but it didn't happen. I saw the panicked look on her face as she scanned Stacey's and my reactions. We smiled big, wooden smiles, but Jessie was clearly freaking out. She asked to get down off the exam table because she couldn't do it herself, and then she sat in my lap and snuggled her head into my arm. I was so frustrated because I knew just what was on Jessie's mind.

The Make-A-Wish woman must have felt very flustered at the reaction. She said, "I'll leave you with some information," and handed us some paperwork and left. She was a nice woman with all the right intentions, just the wrong introduction to give to my daughter. Once she was out of the room, Jessie opened up to us.

"Why is Make-A-Wish here?" she asked.

"Well, honey, I think they just want to do something nice for you ..."

"I'm not dying."

I swallowed hard. "Of course you're not."

"Make-A-Wish is for kids who are dying."

"No, that's not true. It's for kids who are going through big medical challenges, like you are with your tumor."

"I don't want a wish. That should only be for the kids who are dying."

"You don't have to do it, but maybe let's read about what it's all about. It might be really nice."

After giving the medical team a piece of my mind in the hallway — "Please don't ever surprise us like that again without clearing it with us. She is going to look to us for answers, and how are we supposed to give her answers if we don't even know what's happening?" — we finished the exam and headed home.

We could have introduced that so differently, I thought. Stacey and I could have just told her she was getting a wish because it was something they did for all of Dr. Shen's special patients. It didn't have to add to the stress of the day. Jessie was stressed enough. At this point, she was losing her hair in greater volume because of the chemotherapy, and she was getting down about it. It came out in chunks and was hard to brush. When she was just hanging around at home with us, sometimes she didn't bother covering it up, but if there was a possibility she'd see anyone, she wore a beanie cap. It was humiliating to her. Wigs were too uncomfortable and fake-looking on her, but we found her a baseball cap with a fake ponytail attached to it, and that looked more natural.

Seeing her lose all that beautiful blonde hair was tough for us too. We didn't know when — or if — we'd ever see it again. She had finally been weaned off the steroids and her face was not as puffy, but losing her hair made her feel even worse than the "moon face" had. We needed some cheering up, and the Make-A-Wish experience should have fit the bill.

Once Jessie had processed her thoughts and talked it through with us and her siblings, her mood turned around.

"Maybe I could meet the president of the United States!" she said.

"Or you could go to a taping of *Project Runway*," Stacey said. That was another of Jessie's favorite shows.

"Or you could take your dad to a Lakers game," I suggested with a grin. Oh, it was worth a try.

But she eventually nixed the idea of a vacation or a celebrity meeting. "I want something permanent, not just something I can see in pictures later. I want something I can have forever."

The Make-A-Wish representative came back to interview Jessie. One of the rules of the organization is that they interview the children without the parents present so they don't have to worry about a parent influencing the child's wish (there went my Lakers tickets!). They tell the child to name their top three wishes, and when the representative came out afterward to talk to us, she said that Jessie had one top wish—a puppy.

We already had two Labs at the time, but Jessie had her heart set on a puppy of her own. Make-A-Wish could fulfill the wish, but it would take six to eight weeks. When you're dealing with a prognosis of twelve to eighteen months, six to eight weeks is a large chunk of that time. In addition, they couldn't let Jessie pick out the dog she wanted. The organization would pick the dog for her. Jessie asked if she could use some of the money from the swim-a-thon to buy the puppy herself, and we agreed.

We pored over puppy adoption pictures online. Jessie, Shaya, and I each looked on our laptops at different websites. We knew she wanted a Lab, but she wasn't sure what type of Lab. There was a cool-looking gray line that she was checking out, and then Shaya said, "What about white?"

"White?"

We crowded around the computer and saw these terrific white fluff balls. The owner had just two left—one boy and one girl, identifiable by the blue and pink bows. Jessie fell in love with the boy, pointing and saying, "That's the puppy I want!"

The only problem was that he was in Texas, so we had to get him a plane ticket. It was nearly 100 degrees on the day he was slated to fly, and when it's that hot, it's questionable whether a dog can make the trip. We couldn't get in touch with the seller, so we headed out to the airport not knowing if the puppy would be on the scheduled flight. We got to the cargo center and showed our paperwork proving we were the dog's new owners. Then we waited and watched planes land, and, finally, a man pulling a wagon full of boxes and crates called out, "Okay, dog's here."

"He's here!" Jessie said, greeting the curious little ball of fur. She'd brought a bin full of toys for him in the car, and as soon as JT got just a little too cuddly with the pup, Jessie said, "He's *my* dog, not your dog."

Oh, my daughter was wonderful, but she wasn't perfect. She liked to save up her imperfections for her siblings. And sometimes, if they snapped back at her, she'd get a big grin on her face and say, "You have to be nice to me. I'm fragile!"

After getting to know the pup better, she named him Moe — or sometimes Mr. Moe. He was a steadfast companion for her, just the way she'd imagined. Moe followed her around everywhere, sitting on her lap, sleeping with her on the couch, licking her face, playing in the yard with her on good days. It was good for her. We tried to get her outside every day, and so did Nana on the days she was watching Jessie. It became easier to coax her outside when she felt a responsibility to the dog — because dogs need to go out, and they need to get exercise.

She was always more motivated to help others than herself, and that included her dog. She loved throwing a ball into the pool and watching him jump in to retrieve it. Like most other kids, she was a lot more interested in playing with her pets than taking care of the associated chores, which meant she still didn't like cleaning up after him, even on her good days. But Moe was something special — Moe was *hers*, and he seemed to know it right away.

When Jessie would wake up in the morning and come down

the stairs, we'd have to hold him back because he would get so excited to see her that he'd bound over and jump right into her, and her balance wasn't good enough to withstand it. He was such a strong dog right from the start that she wasn't able to walk him on a leash. He'd strain against it hard enough to knock her over.

Every day, she would sit on the couch wearing her beanie, and every day, Moe would stick his nose under it and wriggle it half off. He was always playing with her beanies, and she let him do it.

"Isn't he the cutest little thing?" she'd ask.

"He's terrific," I agreed.

He made her smile. He could have been the mangiest mutt in town and I still would have thought he was terrific. All that mattered was keeping her spirits up.

Instead of providing the puppy, the Make-A-Wish Foundation granted Jessie's second wish—a separate space for her to relax and hang out with her friends. A "fun room," she called it. Their team of designers came over and walked around our house and talked about what Jessie was hoping for. Thankfully, our garage was large enough to hold three cars, so we took one stall and dedicated it to JoyJars. We had outgrown the kitchen and now had shelves full of supplies and a big table for assembly in the garage. Our friends J. Steele and Trent Frum donated their time and expertise to put up a wall to divide the space so the other part of the garage could be used as Jessie's hangout room.

The Make-A-Wish team let Jessie pick the paint colors. She picked one giant wall of chalkboard paint, which was a neat touch. She would go in there and draw on the wall sometimes, and as time went on and people began coming over and helping out, they'd write notes to Jessie on that wall. It's now sealed over so the notes are preserved forever.

To help her improve her balance and encourage her to keep moving, the team put in an Xbox Kinect. She loved the dance games and another game in particular that is modeled after the television show *Wipeout*. It became a form of physical therapy for her, forcing her to balance on one leg, jump, and dodge obstacles. Her physical therapist even sweetened the deal by promising to give her a massage for every thirty minutes of Xbox she played. Imagine bribing a child to play video games! But this was an active and difficult challenge for her, even though it was also fun. It was a thrill when she discovered one day that she could stand on one leg again—amazing how many things we take for granted and how many reasons we can find to celebrate when even the smallest thing goes right.

Thank you, God, for helping Jessie balance today. Thank you for giving her the confidence to try. Thank you for this wonderful team of helpers who made it possible.

On top of everything else, the Make-A-Wish team put in a sixty-five-inch flat-screen television, a foosball game, a craft table, and big floor pillows. It was perfect. They did a great job making it comfortable, fun, and kid friendly. And just one wall over from the Joy Factory.

Mondays became our day to work on the JoyJars in that garage. Jessie figured that if all those sweet notes from strangers helped to "soften her edges," then these JoyJars could help to soften the edges for the other kids fighting cancer.

It was just the two of us on some days, and on other days, friends or family helped us stuff the jars. The first time Kimmy helped, Jessie became quite a taskmaster, shaking her head and pointing out how she was doing it all wrong.

"Kimmy, Kimmy, Kimmy. See this? This is cheesy. No kid wants this," she said, pulling out a pointless little doodad. Of course she was right. There were companies that made whole assortments of useless trinkets for piñatas, grab bags, and such. Those toys were *not allowed* in Jessie's JoyJars. Then she demonstrated how to better situate each item so more things could fit into the jar. Ah, what a great business leader she would have made.

When we finished, she admired our handiwork.

"Every kid fighting cancer should get one of these," she said.

"Every kid?"

She nodded.

I guess I could have just smiled and patted her head, but I didn't. I took it as a directive. This is what would make my daughter happy and fulfill her dream, and she was too young to figure out the logistics of it on her own—so that's what I had to set out to do.

Every kid was a huge goal. An almost unthinkably huge goal. Every weekday in the United States, forty-six kids are diagnosed with cancer, more than thirteen thousand per year.* Add that to the number of kids who continue to fight cancer year after year, and we find there are approximately 200,000 kids fighting cancer in and out of hospitals just in this country. And since love doesn't know any borders, why would we stick to just this country? More than 500,000 kids are fighting cancer world-wide. We can't even gauge reliable numbers because there are so many poverty-stricken countries without established health care systems, so their numbers don't get counted—and those kids aren't often even diagnosed or treated.

There was no way we were going to be able to afford to stuff 500,000 JoyJars with our savings and our bake sales. We were just a little local operation nowhere near on track to get to those

---

*See American Childhood Cancer Organization, "Childhood Cancer Statistics," www.acco.org/Information/AboutChildhoodCancer/Childhood CancerStatistics.aspx (accessed January 2, 2014).

kinds of numbers. If we were going to do this, we were going to have to get bigger. Draw more attention, apply for grants, find sponsors. Yes, it was a big goal, but we had a bigger God. Through him, all things are possible.

I was helpless to stop the cancer cells that had invaded my daughter's body, but this was the one area where I was not helpless at all. I could and would help my daughter fulfill her mission.

lonely, limited, and labeled

When Nana watched Jessie, she tried to follow our lead and keep things as normal as possible. That meant, among other things, trying to keep up with all the things a sixth grader would normally do if she weren't going through cancer.

For the remainder of the sixth-grade year, Jessie's teachers would drop off schoolwork, and we'd do it with her and turn it in for her—projects, essays, reports, everything. Stacey and Nana were homeschooling her, technically, though have you seen sixth-grade math lately? With all the new standards and curriculums, it's nothing like getting back on a bicycle after not riding for a long time; it's more like traveling to another planet and attempting to communicate with extraterrestrials. Although Jessie was not at the very top of her class, she was in the gifted and talented program, so her homework was even more challenging.

Early on in treatments, Jessie couldn't even hold a pencil, which was hard for her to deal with because she took schoolwork so seriously. But she got her grip back, completed all her work, and was invited to the sixth-grade graduation ceremony in June. She had been back to school only once since her treatments had started—to present a project at open house night. Each of the kids in her class had to invent a civilization and make a display and a report about it. Jessie's civilization was called "Foodopia," and another kid in the class created a "NEGU Island" civilization—what an honor! Graduation was something we were all hopeful about, as long as she could stay healthy enough to handle it.

Jessie's blood work hadn't been perfect in the weeks leading up to the graduation. Her blood sugar, hemoglobin, and platelets were all abnormal, and she needed to go for a two-hour blood transfusion in May that was supposed to help restore her energy, though she didn't feel much different afterward. When they retested a week later, though, she was out of the danger zone.

She talked about going back to swimming practice in "a few weeks." I didn't have the heart to tell her that wouldn't happen, though she was at least aware she wouldn't be strong enough to race again for a while. I looked at her some days and wondered if she'd ever be strong enough again—and then I forced those thoughts out of my head. There was still a chance. She could be in that 1 percent.

In the meantime, she stopped by the pool from time to time when Stacey needed to drop things off or pick things up. She'd leave notes on her coaches' desks, like: "Hi, Coach Bryan! How are you? Looks like it's going to rain today. Hope you don't get too wet. Love, Jessie."

Every spring, the Nadadores swim team took a weekend trip to compete at Clovis High School in Fresno, California, bringing sixty younger athletes and sixty older athletes who were strong competitors. Jessie and Shaya had both competed at Clovis the previous year. Of course, Jessie couldn't compete this year, but Shaya was chosen to go in the older group, and Jessie really wanted to accompany her to cheer her on. The team was traveling by bus without their parents—just coaches and chaperones (luckily, Stacey was one of the chaperones)—to give the kids a taste of what it would be like to compete professionally, but that was out of the question for Jessie.

In the end, we agreed to let Kimmy make the trip with her. They drove in Tanta's supernice Tahoe behind the team bus and then got a hotel room together with Stacey while Shaya roomed with the other girls. During the day, Kimmy and Jessie shopped and watched movies and had precious bonding time away from treatments and the realities that came with life at home. Jessie loved getting to spend so much "alone time" with her aunt and getting to see her swim friends and coaches again. The team did well in competitions, and they played at an arcade afterward, where several kids pooled their tickets and won a giant stuffed bear for Jessie.

The trip was bittersweet. She felt pretty good while she was there and didn't tire out too quickly, and she enjoyed getting away from home and spending time with her friends again. But it also reminded her of what she was missing out on.

"I just miss being a normal twelve-year-old kid," she wrote when she got back. "I miss being able to run around and not worrying about what I'm eating, drinking, or doing."

Her emotions were up and down after the trip. She had long been telling me she felt lonely and limited, and now she added another word to the list—*labeled*. She hated the fact that she had to wear the "sick kid" label. It wasn't anybody's fault. No one treated her badly or purposely made her feel alienated, but some things are obvious just by the way people look at someone or what they *don't* say.

I looked for ways to cheer her up and encourage her to keep focusing on the positive, and other people often helped with that goal. JT did it just by being his silly self. He knew he could always get a laugh out of her by lifting his shirt and doing his famous "belly waves."

Other people offered slightly more serious help. Once a month at Saddleback, there was a special "night of worship," and Pastor Buddy Owens asked if we'd bring Jessie in June for a whole night to be focused on her. She agreed as long as she didn't have to talk! They played the CBS video to introduce Jessie and her story, leaving many in tears. Then we came out onstage with the choir behind us, and Pastor Buddy spoke. He laid hands on her and asked the congregation of about three thousand people to pray for her healing. Everyone raised their hands toward Jessie—it was such a powerful moment.

He said, in part, *"We bring our little sister Jessie to you, and we ask you to be merciful. You've told us over and over that you're a God of mercy and compassion, and we're asking tonight, Lord, would you once again be merciful? Would you once again be compassionate? We've seen you time and time again bring healing and restoration, and so we're asking, Lord, would you just one more time do it again? We ask you, Father, would you please heal Jessie's body? Would you restore her to perfect health? Would you raise her up as a testimony to the healing power of Jesus Christ? Lord, would you bless her with health and strength and vitality?*

"We pray, Father, for her family, that you would strengthen their faith and their love for one another. That you would hold all of them and let them know beyond any doubt how much you care and how present you are in their home and their lives right now. Surround them, Lord, with people who love them. Surround them with your presence. Fill them with your Holy

Spirit, and empower them, Lord, to walk in faithfulness, to follow after you. Would you give them wisdom in every decision they make for Jessie's care? Would you watch over every step they take? Lord God Almighty, we ask you in the name of Jesus Christ for a miracle of healing in Jessie's body. Only you can do this, Lord, and so we turn to you. Would you please do what only you can do?"

Soon afterward, Jessie was chosen to receive an award from Kingdom Assignment at their annual celebration event. The event that year was to take place close to our home at Crossline Community Church. In November 2000, the leaders of Kingdom Assignment, Pastor Denny Bellesi and his wife, Leesa, handed out $100 bills to a hundred members of their congregation and told them it was God's money and they were to "multiply it." They told the congregation it was a "kingdom assignment" — which became the name of their movement. They challenged people to use their God-given talents, treasures, and time in the service of others to advance God's kingdom globally. Each year, they give out "Well Done Awards" at an annual celebration to people who captured the spirit of the movement.

The name of the awards comes from the parable of the bags of gold in Matthew 25:21, where the servant's master says to him, "Well done, good and faithful servant! You have been faithful with a few things; I will put you in charge of many things. Come and share your master's happiness!"

Jessie was one of the award recipients in 2011, along with *American Idol* contestant Colton Dixon and *iCarly* actor Noah Munck. Our family, plus several family friends, teachers, and Shaya's friends, attended the celebration, where Jessie received an engraved plaque. She loved meeting the other two honorees as well. *iCarly* is a big deal in the twelve-year-old world.

When graduation time came around two weeks later, Jessie

wasn't in the best shape. She had just fought off a cough and was feeling particularly weak and tired. Some days, she took three or even four naps. The day before the ceremony, she had her blood work done at CHOC and found out her blood counts were low. They were just on the cusp of being dangerously low, where we'd have to stop her chemo until the counts came back up; this would make it possible for the tumor to grow.

"Can she still go to graduation?" I asked the doctor.

"Yes, as long as she wears a mask and doesn't stay to socialize before or after. She should show up right before the names are called and go home after receiving her diploma."

Knowing that, we left the final decision with Jessie, though we had already suspected what might happen. She had been shying away from going out with us to run errands, even when she was physically feeling okay. When we talked her into getting out for just a little while to go to the smoothie shop or the scrapbooking store with Nana, she'd say, "I hope we don't run into anyone I know."

But the thing is, lots of people knew Jessie now. She might not have known everyone around town, but many of them knew her because of Facebook, articles in the newspaper about JoyJars, the CBS show, posters for the swim-a-thon. She was pretty easily recognizable, especially because of her Scotch-taped glasses and her beanie caps.

"Hey, you're Jessie, aren't you? I saw you on the news the other day," someone would say.

She'd smile and nod and say thank you when they wished her well, but that was about all they'd get out of her. She felt terrible about the way she looked and shy about the attention, so she did all she could to make herself invisible. People have described her as wise beyond her years and an old soul, and all of that is true, but she was also a normal preteen girl who cared about her appearance. Sometimes it took all of her energy just to run those errands and put on a smile and make small talk for a minute. Knowing that, it wasn't too surprising that she decided not to attend her graduation ceremony. She just wasn't feeling up to it. We did find out afterward that there was a big round of applause when her name was called.

It was a hard decision for her to make, but the NEGU Nation reminded her that she had a bigger goal—fighting cancer.

And my little superhero devoted herself to that goal whole-heartedly. That same week marked our first monetary donation to CHOC. We had raised $500 toward cancer research, and Jessie presented the check to the doctors so proudly. She also brought in another twenty four JoyJars for Jaime and the nurses to distribute to their patients, bringing her total up to 275 Joy-Jars delivered. That was a big deal for us at the time. Jessie's milestone goal was to distribute five hundred JoyJars. We had no idea how thoroughly we'd smash that goal. Off they went, little packages of love—because when you're feeling lonely, limited, and labeled, the best antidote is love.

After months away from swimming, Jessie was excited to find she was able to do a few laps in our pool that June. Some of her strength had returned, and she wasn't as dizzy or weak anymore. This was the beginning of what we'd come to term "the honeymoon period." She never returned to her old normal self completely, but she was able to get up and around much more than before. Soon, she didn't need to reach for our hands when she walked. She didn't even need to put her hands out to steady herself. We watched her run and jump in the backyard with Moe, and it was wonderful to see. The double vision still tripped her up if she took off her glasses, but it was worlds away from where we'd been just a month earlier.

Thank you, God.

She began swimming in our backyard pool regularly again, always wearing a T-shirt and sunblock because both the radiation and steroids made her skin highly sensitive and prone to sunburns. Before that, she had rarely bothered with sunblock because her naturally olive skin tanned beautifully and never burned. But she put up with the additional measures easily, considering the trade-off was getting back a piece of her identity. She loved being in the water.

It was time to open up her world a little more again. It had been quite a while since she'd seen her best friend, Sophie, from the swimming team. They didn't go to the same elementary school but were so excited by the plan to start seventh grade in the same middle school the following September. Sophie kept in contact with Jessie nearly every day by texts, comments online, or phone calls, and the day finally came when Jessie felt ready to hang out again. She invited Sophie over for a sleepover.

The two of them went in the pool together early in the evening. Jessie had lost a lot of hair by that point, and being in the water just accentuated it—making her hairline look receded and emphasizing how thin and sparse the remaining hair was. If she felt self-conscious about it, she wore a swim cap, but with our family and with Sophie, she felt comfortable enough to leave it off. After swimming, the two of them just hung around outside and talked for a while before coming in.

The plan was for them to watch a movie, do some crafts, and just be silly together as usual. Then Sophie disappeared into the bathroom for a good length of time. Eventually, Stacey knocked on the door to check on her.

"Soph? Are you okay?"

"Yeah," she called back. "I just miss my dad. He's been traveling and just got back. I think I want to go home."

"Oh. Okay, we can call him."

When Sophie emerged, she looked shaken, and we could see she'd been crying. It wasn't hard to tell this wasn't about missing her dad, though I wished Jessie had believed that. I knew something was wrong, but I didn't know exactly what it was. Sophie went home that night, and the next day her mom talked to Stacey about it.

"I'm so sorry, Stacey. Sophie just had a really hard time seeing Jessie that way."

The hair, the glasses, the moon face that hadn't really gone away, the weight loss, all of it—she didn't look like Jessie anymore, and for her twelve-year-old best friend, it was just too emotional. It made everything real, and not just like a bad illness she'd soon get over. I understood. We love Sophie, and she'd been a wonderful friend to Jessie since they'd met. I knew they would remain special friends—and they did, getting back to texting and online messaging instead of seeing each other in person—but I also knew how hurt Jessie was going to feel, and I hated that it was one more thing I couldn't shield her from.

Sophie had been one of Jessie's last remaining close friends who didn't shy away from her. It was so awkward for all of them, most of whom had very limited life experience with things like cancer and side effects from chemotherapy. It was much easier for adults to say the "right" things. There was no shortage of grown-ups writing, calling, and sending her things, but her face lit up extra enthusiastically when she heard from kids.

Jessie was down about it, but she was never depressed. She would get sad for a little while, but she'd always pull herself out of it again. Sometimes it was a Bible verse that would help clear things up for her, like one of her favorites, Philippians 4:13: "I can do all things through Christ who strengthens me."

She would pray for strength, and I knew she didn't just mean physical strength.

In July, we found out that one of the first kids Jessie had Joy Mobbed had gone to heaven. Hailey was a little girl who had just turned eight years old and was fighting acute lymphoblastic leukemia — a rare cancer that can often be fatal within months. In Hailey's case, that was true. She was diagnosed in April, and her battle ended on July 28. She was one of the first kids with cancer to whom we sent a JoyJar outside of our area — she lived in Boston.

It was far from the last time we'd see that happen. So many of "our" kids — the ones we sent JoyJars to, the ones we Joy Mobbed — would end up going to heaven. I thought it was important not to hide that reality from Jessie, but not to dwell on it either. I would tell her things matter-of-factly and gauge her reaction.

"Hey, honey, I have something to tell you. You remember Hailey from Boston? Well, she lost her battle yesterday, and she's gone to heaven to be with Jesus."

"Oh, that's so sad. I hope her family is okay," Jessie said.

She didn't personalize it. She never once said to me, "Is that going to happen to me?" I'm so thankful she didn't, because of all the answers I practiced in my head, none were perfect. I thought about how I'd respond if her health declined and she asked me if she was dying.

"Well, sweet pea," I might say, "all of us will go to heaven someday. We don't really die. We stay alive in heaven. None of us know when. You may go there sooner than me, but we'll all be together again soon."

It was the best I could do for her. I knew her faith was strong and hoped it would be enough to ease her anxiety. I hated thinking about losing Jessie, but what made it so much harder was thinking about how terrifying it would be for her.

I often sent words of support and even personal videos to

grieving parents. I didn't necessarily feel like I was looking into my own future except when I spoke with fellow "DIPG parents." There were several who had reached out to me by e-mail and phone, like my friend Stephen Czech in Connecticut, whose son Mikey had lost his battle four years earlier. Mikey had been diagnosed with DIPG on his eleventh birthday, January 6, 2008, and fought valiantly through a clinical trial similar to the one Jessie went through that—at least initially—seemed to work very well for him. His tumor shrunk by an astonishing 85 percent, and he entered into a honeymoon phase like Jessie's for four months.

Mikey went back to his normal life, which included lots of sports. He even went to Yankee Stadium and became an honorary batboy for a day, as arranged by Make-A-Wish. But then cysts began growing in the voids where the tumors had shrunk, putting pressure on his cranial nerves. That led to the same sorts of symptoms the tumors caused. Quickly, he was unable to walk, felt numbness on his right side, and had trouble swallowing. He went to heaven on September 7, just eight months after his diagnosis.

Kathleen O'Connell was another big source of support for me. Kathleen was a producer for *48 Hours* in New York and a friend of Lisa Sigell's at CBS. When we taped our CBS segment, Lisa had told me about Kathleen, who'd recently lost her thirteen-year-old son to DIPG. Of course, it's always difficult to hear that DIPG has claimed another child's life, but what was encouraging to me was that Lucas had lived for twenty-two months. I was enough of a realist by then to understand that DIPG would probably take Jessie from us too, but twenty-two months sounded pretty good to me—better than the twelve to eighteen months doctors had predicted for Jessie.

Kathleen had pulled out all the stops in helping Lucas fight his battle. He had a whole medical team behind him, and she had spent massive amounts of money consulting the best doctors and nutritionists around. She knew all sorts of people and was able to help us make connections and get appointments, as well as suggesting things to try with Jessie, like protein injections.

This is a woman who thinks outside the box, I thought. We did all the traditional things we were supposed to do with Jessie, but also added complementary therapies and supplements. She especially liked acupuncture, which relaxed her. The acupuncturist, Ruth, was the wife of a pediatric neurosurgeon at CHOC, so she had worked with several kids we knew from the hospital, and parents had told us she was good at getting kids to relax after treatments. She burned incense during the sessions, which Jessie liked so much that we took her out to pick out incense to burn at home. She picked sandalwood and ocean.

I thought to myself that Kathleen had probably extended her son's life by several months because of all the "extra" things she did to help his body fight the disease. She became a role model for me, and I checked in with her every six to eight weeks to tell her how things were going and to ask for advice.

Just like Jessie now had her clan of courageous kids fighting cancer, these were "my people." They were the parents who'd already fought this battle and could tell me more about what to expect as we waited to see what was coming around the bend next. Long before it happened for us, I knew all about various side effects and when to expect them, what the honeymoon phase would be like, and the sad reminder that this phase wouldn't last forever.

Sometimes that summer, we could forget for just a few moments at a time. Watching Jessie run around with JT, like she always did before, or put on a fashion show with Shaya or laugh with her cousins in the pool ...

"Look at you!" I'd tell her sometimes. "You're kicking this tumor's butt!"

That's what she believed too. She told us she'd never have to go into the third phase of treatment (the one I called "trick") because we were all praying for the tumor to be gone, and she trusted it would be.

While we were barbecuing in the yard one day, T looked at me and said, "She's doing *so* well. She looks so good." The unsaid thing was, "Why does this have to end?"

In the midst of this wonderful respite came one of the starkest reminders of what was to come. One day, Jessie's doctor handed me a stack of business cards and pamphlets and said, "This is for you to look over. It's best to start this process now."

It was literature from hospice providers.

My younger daughter was running and swimming and dancing—and we were supposed to make a decision about who would care for her in her final hours. We were just coming up for air for the first time in months—and we were supposed to think ahead to the time when we'd be drowning. There's nothing quite like terminal cancer to suck the joy right out of a room.

"Interview several of them and choose the one you're most comfortable with," the doctor said.

Do *what*? It was as absurd as it sounded, but all I could say was, "Okay, thanks." The hospital couldn't choose for us, so I had to make phone calls to various hospice providers and make appointments for them to come to my office and put on presentations to sell me on their services. They had websites and promotional videos depicting dying children and crying parents, then smiling people holding hands with their nurses. What a concept to have to sell like any other business—like a landscaper or plumber!

How do you choose such a thing? I had to ask the craziest questions:

Will my daughter suffer?

What will you do for her if she is in pain?

What can you do to make her transition to heaven easier?

What will her final hours look like?

Do you stay with us overnight?

What happens after she passes?

They'd tell me their answers, and then I'd say, "Okay, thanks," and the next provider would walk in for another interview. It was one of the hardest, most heartless experiences of the whole ordeal, even though all of the providers were polite and my best friend, Jeff, sat with me through all the interviews. In the end, Stacey and I chose TrinityKids Care, which is solely dedicated to infants and kids with terminal illnesses.

Right after we hired them, they began visiting Jessie. The idea was for Jessie and our family to get comfortable with her hospice team so it wouldn't be a shock when strangers showed up at the end. They spent time getting to know her and check on her symptoms so they'd know how to best offer comfort and support when they were needed.

I didn't want Jessie to ever hear the words *hospice* or *palliative care* or anything along those lines, so we called the women who came to visit "Dr. Shen's traveling nurses." We explained that Dr. Shen had a heavy caseload and couldn't do it all herself, so she sometimes sent out a team of traveling nurses to check on her patients. Jessie responded well to this and didn't seem stressed about our new visitors. For me, it was another layer of the veil between reality and what I could share with our kids. We never ever wanted Jessie to lose hope—hope of a miracle, hope of eighteen months, hope that seventh grade was a possibility, hope that she could race again. Without hope, there is nothing.

When Jessie was nervous about her MRIs, I asked her to remember to trust God. We talked about Proverbs 3:5–6, which reads, "Trust in the LORD with all your heart and lean not on your own understanding; in all your ways submit to him, and he will make your paths straight." It was something I still needed to remember too. It was so hard *not* to lean on my own understanding, but we are not expected to understand God's plan fully while we're here on earth. There had to be a reason for Jessie's cancer, but it wasn't for us to know yet.

Her MRI at the end of June showed another very small reduction in her tumor, and the one in July showed no change. As long as it wasn't increasing, that was a good thing. Even so, most of the tumor was still there, and doctors had already told us they could not do any more radiation. Any level of radiation, no matter how small, has the possibility of *causing* cancer. Researchers try to determine an "acceptable risk" level when they're using it to *treat* cancer, and then doctors don't exceed that level. So our only medical hope now was the chemotherapy, which hadn't yet made a significant difference on its own. As we all celebrated the Fourth of July in our backyard, I couldn't help but think this would probably be our last time celebrating this holiday with Jessie.

But wouldn't it be awesome if we could make it to the next one? All of us together, just like this. Mr. Moe would probably double in size by then. Maybe Jessie's hair would have grown back in. She would have finished the seventh grade at her big new school, would be back on the swim team ...

She came with me to cheer on Shaya at the Junior Olympics again that summer, and we set up a TeamNEGU booth where we sold NEGU merchandise and JoyJars. At that time, the model was that for every JoyJar someone bought to give to someone they knew (which came with a NEGU T-shirt and wristband, but was otherwise empty, to be stuffed by the gift giver), we could then send a JoyJar to a kid with cancer. The requested amount was $40, enough to cover the expenses of both jars. Jessie was an enthusiastic participant both at the booth and in the bleachers. When Shaya struggled, Jessie sucked in her breath with concern, and when Shaya finished in the top eight, Jessie clapped and cheered.

It was easy to think in those days that this did not look like a dying girl — just any other girl cheering on a sibling, albeit with some strange glasses. But inevitably, something would bring me back to reality and back to my role as the planner, the researcher, the daddy still desperately searching for a cure where none existed.

I would get into arguments regularly with the case manager, doctors, and nurses because they were unwilling to try new things. One thing that held us back was that DIPG tumors were almost never biopsied because of the risk of the procedure (which could include serious complications like hemorrhaging), and yet a biopsy could yield more information about the tumor and give a better idea of how to treat it. At this point, nobody really knows whether or not DIPG tumors differ from child to child, and, obviously, nobody has come up with an effective way of treating them. Our doctors had never mentioned doing a biopsy, and when I brought it up, they said no.

"You're telling me my daughter is going to die — yes or no?"

"Yes."

"Then what do we have to lose? Why in the world wouldn't you try something that might help her and provide information that helps other kids with DIPG?"

"Mr. Rees, we have protocols to follow ..."

"The protocol means my daughter is going to die in a few months! I need you to think differently about this because I'm not willing to accept the status quo. You're offering us treatments that you know aren't going to save her, or even extend her life by much. So let's try something else!"

"I know this is difficult, but please calm down. There are strict regulations about what we can do. Our hands are tied."

I decided to find someone whose hands were untied. I was tired of hearing about insurance companies and funding and approvals and classifications. When something isn't working, you don't just keep doing it. All I wanted was to hear someone say, "Let's try something new."

Doctors don't tell you everything when you're dealing with pediatric cancer. They tell you about the things they're approved to do, which mostly means things that the Children's Oncology Group (COG) recommends because they've already been tried (and, uniformly, have failed at doing anything more than extending a child's life by a few months). One thing I learned along this path was not to give up control of my daughter's treatments. I knew that if I just obeyed everything the doctors told me, then my daughter would die, just as all of their previous patients had done. Were they even really looking for a cure? Or were they content to just keep trying the same old things that didn't work because it was too much trouble to get approvals and funding to try something that hadn't been tried before?

I was praying and reading and reaching out of my comfort zone to consider things I'd never have imagined. Shots in the dark, I knew, but maybe there was a vaccine or a different type of chemo that no one had tried on DIPG yet. Maybe a faith healer could help us, or a special vitamin. People suggested all kinds of things, from particular vegetables to "miracle" doctors, and I diligently researched and implemented many of those things into our routine. We took Jessie to a group of elders for laying on of hands, as James urges in the Bible. We also made her drink special water with high alkalinity (a pH greater than 7) because a friend suggested that this type of water can absorb the free radicals coursing through the body and correct excess acidity—and if you believe the claims, cancer cells can't survive in an alkaline environment. Snake oil? Yes, it probably is. But just like the marketers hope, people in our situation will try just about anything. If you'd told me that standing on my head and singing "The Star-Spangled Banner" could cure her cancer, I might have tried that too. At least privately.

Stacey and I were doing all we could to keep Jessie's hope alive. Now we needed a doctor who would help keep ours alive.

kona

I finally got my wish in August when I found a surgeon at Stanford University Medical Center willing to do a biopsy of Jessie's tumor. There were no guarantees that it would do us any good, of course, and he even warned me of the possibility they could go through the trouble of cutting into her brain and come up with only dead tissue that had already been knocked out by the radiation. But still, he was willing to try when no one else would.

We scheduled the biopsy for September. While things were still going so well, we wanted to take a big family vacation all together—the biggest and best our family had ever had.

"If you could pick anywhere, where would you want to go?" I asked Jessie.

"Hawaii," she said.

"I'll see what I can do."

So Hawaii it would be. I knew of just the place, if we could manage it. I had once been to a beautiful resort with Pastor Rick to meet with people. It was called Kukio, and it was a private oceanfront club and residential community in Kona where almost all of the guests are millionaires or beyond. The general manager there was a friend of mine whose sister worked at Saddleback. I reached out to him and asked, "Would you help us create an amazing experience for Jessie?"

He contacted the resort's owner, who offered us his private home. He has seventeen resorts around the world and told us there was a ten-day span when he wouldn't be at his home at Kukio—and no one else would be either. Lance Armstrong had recently stayed there, and the week after we left, it would be occupied by Pete Sampras and his family. But for those ten days, that house was all ours—Stacey, Shaya, Jessie, JT, Nana, Papa, Kimmy, T, and me.

Before we left on the trip, I e-mailed everyone to say it was important that we make this the best family vacation we'd ever had. It wasn't hard for the family to understand what I really meant by that. I was intimating that this would likely be our last big vacation together with Jessie.

And once again, our wonderful community rose to the occasion. When they learned about our trip, several members of the church donated their frequent flier miles to the cause and covered our airfare. Everyone knew about our upcoming trip—the staff at CHOC, the hospice team, the swim team—and sent us off with happy wishes and a good feeling in our hearts.

Kimmy and T flew out from Denver first, and the rest of us left from Los Angeles. We didn't have the best start when we arrived at security. They made Jessie take off her baseball cap, which she obviously didn't want to do. She had never exposed her balding head to anyone outside of her family, and it humiliated her to the point of tears. But after that moment, we were treated like VIPs. United Airlines' Red Carpet Club lounge is reserved for members who are frequent travelers, and although

I was one, the rest of our crew wasn't. I asked the attendant if maybe I could just bring Jessie in there to rest so she'd be away from the hubbub of the rest of the airport. A few minutes later, another representative from United arrived and said, "Mr. Rees?"

"Yes?"

"Please follow me."

She escorted our whole family to the International Red Carpet Club lounge — and I'd never seen anything like it in an airport. It was a spectacular room with a big television and all you can eat of really good food, not the typical airline pretzels and peanuts. To top it off, there were hardly any other people there, so we had room to spread out and talk. What a great way to start our vacation, feeling like royalty.

We all had first-class tickets on the plane, and when we stepped out onto the tarmac upon landing, Kimmy and T were there already to greet us with leis. Then we traveled to Kukio, which was even more beautiful than I'd remembered. Private, white-sand beaches stretched as far as we could see, with glistening turtles climbing out of the water and along the sand.

We spent time as a family lounging around the pool and playing on the beach. Jessie didn't go in the water much except on my back, but she had never been much of an ocean girl anyway. One of her favorite swimming coaches, Bryan, had worked hard to get her to push past her fears one day when they had waded out into the water at the beach back home.

"That's far enough," she told him. And he said, "Let's just go a little farther." She grasped his hand and trusted him, taking just one more step than she thought she could, and then another. It was the same kind of quiet bravery she had shown all throughout her cancer battle.

Over the course of our vacation, we'd break off into smaller groups often. Some of us went canoeing or snorkeling, while I hung back with Jessie. She preferred to wear her baseball cap and stay away from situations where she'd have to expose her nearly bald head. Other times, Jessie went with her mom and Kimmy to get massages, manicures, and pedicures at the spa. I went off with T to play golf. Jessie and Shaya joined us one day. Jessie couldn't wait to drive a golf cart, and when she did, she drove it straight into a sand trap because she didn't brake in time.

We went on all kinds of day trips, including one to Ocean Rider Seahorse Farm, where we learned that the males carry the eggs, not the females. We got to see different varieties of seahorses in various stages, and at the end, we could dip our freshly washed and sanitized hands into a tank to have a seahorse wrap its tail around our fingers. Strange and cool.

All the women went to Tiffany's one day just to browse, because it was *Tiffany's*. Then they spotted one table of jewelry that was less expensive than the rest, and Jessie fixed her gaze on a little heart necklace. Every one of them ended up buying matching heart jewelry in little blue Tiffany's boxes. We took pictures of them together, and it became a very special memory. It was all about unity, family, and love.

Swimming with dolphins was another special memory. We were told to swim out to the middle of a clear blue lagoon and float there while waiting for the dolphins to interact with us. Jessie didn't feel comfortable swimming out that far, so she stayed about waist-deep in the water with the instructor and helped to give the hand signals to the dolphins. We didn't push Jessie. So much control had already been taken away from her that we decided whatever made her comfortable was the right thing.

Two days before we left on the trip, she began complaining of difficulty swallowing again, so we had rushed her in for a checkup—worried that the tumor might be growing—but the doctor assured her it was a psychological block and not a physical one. He even showed her the X-rays proving that everything was working fine. It was still leftover fear from the big choking episode.

"God is good," she said, echoing a statement she'd heard me say many times. She was relieved there was no true choking danger, but even knowing that didn't resolve the phobia for her. I thought we'd be able to tempt her with the exotic foods in Hawaii, but it didn't happen. She wouldn't eat solid foods, so she missed out on the wonderful cuisine—but she had soups, protein shakes, and fresh fruit smoothies she said were the best.

We had to camouflage the fact that she wasn't eating when we went to the nightly luaus. She didn't want the chefs to feel bad or the people around us to ask why she wasn't taking any food, so it became almost a joke. We'd all stick things on Jessie's plate at the buffet that we wanted to eat, and then we'd covertly steal everything back off her plate once we were at the table.

"How's the mahimahi? It looks so good," she said.

"It is. Are you sure you don't want just a little taste?" Kimmy asked.

She shook her head and smiled. She just wanted to know that the rest of us were enjoying our food.

The only food she ate that halfway counted were the ice cream sandwiches. At the comfort shacks along the golf course, they had delicious handmade ice cream sandwiches that Shaya and Jessie loved.

Along with the eating problems, the only other dose of reality came in the middle of the trip when we had to have a visiting nurse do a blood draw on Jessie, since she couldn't go for her checkup at CHOC. It wasn't Jaime, I'll tell you that. Drawing blood from Jessie was increasingly difficult as her veins collapsed and grew weak from so many "pokes." That morning was a particularly bad one, and it sidelined several of us. Watching Jessie suffer in the middle of paradise was a kick in the teeth. But as usual, once it was over, she moved right on. She didn't complain but just got right back to loving her family and enjoying her vacation.

Jessie spent time with the resort owner's assistant, Jodi, and even brought her a JoyJar one day and told her all about the NEGU Foundation. The following day, Jodi showed up and turned over her arm to reveal a brand-new NEGU tattoo on the inside of her wrist.

"Your daughter has changed my life forever," she told Stacey and me.

It was stunning. Jessie thought it was the greatest thing ever. And we were so humbled that this woman who had known Jessie for such a short period of time made such a commitment to her message. Now the NEGU message would spread to Hawaii—to every person who asked Jodi, "What does your tattoo mean?" It was more proof of what kind of an impact one little girl could have. To us, she was a daughter, a sister, a granddaughter, a niece. Of course we thought she was terrific, but we were always blown away when strangers told us how Jessie inspired them. It was happening more and more lately.

* * *

The sunsets were beautiful, and the weather was perfect. We never wanted our vacation to end. If, as Proverbs 17:22 reads, "a cheerful heart is good medicine," then this trip was good medicine for all of us.

"This was the best family vacation we ever had," Jessie said as it drew to a close.

And she was right.

We came home on a high, thanking God for blessing us generously. We had albums full of photos and memory cards full of videos that would help bring us back to this precious place when we needed to remember.

Jessie thanked God for an amazing trip. Her faith trumped my own on many days. She was the one whose childhood was being stolen by a terrible disease, and yet she felt blessed. She never once grew angry with God for allowing this to happen to her. She didn't ask, "Why me?" or get frustrated with him when he didn't answer her prayers for the next MRI to show no tumor.

I can't say the same.

I did feel upset with God. I wrestled with myself between wanting answers and knowing that God doesn't need to explain himself to me. The praise didn't fall as easily from my lips when I felt this scorned. I wanted to do right by him, but I also wanted him to do right by me.

As soon as we returned home, it was back to the same routine of tests, injections, and doctor meetings. Her magnesium levels went a little crazy, leading to an EKG and a few days where she was not allowed to receive chemo. The MRI that month again showed that the tumor was stable—no growth, no reduction. Disappointing, but we'd take it.

My brother, his wife, and their three kids came to visit us from Oregon at the end of the month, and Jessie had a great time playing with the kids. They mostly hung around the house and the pool with us, but that's all kids need. They dared each other to dive in the pool while doing crazy moves (Jackie Chan kicks, the chicken dance, jumping jacks). They were loud and silly and everything that cousins should be together, and we were sad to see them go. Each of the three of them was perfectly matched in age with our kids. Shaya, Jessie, and JT each had a counterpart in Oregon born within six months of them—Taylor, Emily, and Julia. Although they typically saw each other only once a year, they always quickly picked up where they had left off.

As the summer drew to a close and the new school year approached, we again had to face the question with Jessie: Did she want to go back to school? Really, we didn't care. Education, while important, just didn't have the same meaning in Jessie's life as it would for our other kids. We cared more about her learning how to train her puppy and play Dance Connect than the history of World War I. We just wanted whatever would make her feel happiest.

Germs were a factor, of course. Her immune system was still compromised by the chemo, and catching whatever little viruses were going around could derail her treatment. But for her, again it came down to comfort. She had practically no hair, and she didn't want to wear a wig. When she pictured what it would be like to start at a new school, she imagined kids staring at her and judging her or feeling sorry for her—and that's not what she wanted. So we picked up her books, and once again, Stacey and Nana prepared to homeschool her while Shaya started her first year of high school, another big milestone.

Hair grows back, we reminded Jess. Maybe she'd be ready for school in another couple of months. In the meantime, she'd still socialize with her friends and work on the NEGU Foundation with me. I loved telling her whenever a new sponsor signed on. Pura Vida Bracelets was one of the next to join, making custom waterproof bracelets in the NEGU colors and donating to the foundation $1 for every bracelet sold. Then there was the Tuttle-Click car dealership, which ran a special Facebook promotion for the foundation: For every one of our fans who Liked their page, they'd donate $1 to us, up to $3,000. We got there in no time. Jessie would get so excited whenever another company took an interest in helping her fulfill her dream.

Yes, it was a terrific summer. At least, as terrific as it gets when you still have the ever-looming threat of incurable cancer over your head. But comparatively speaking, it was the best we could have hoped for. We had no way of predicting that the honeymoon period was about to come to a screeching halt.

september

Two of our strongest supporters in recent months had been Ronnie and Toni Andrews, a couple who heard about Jessie's story through people from church. Ronnie was the CEO of Clarient, a local company focused on cancer diagnostics and molecular pathology, and two church leaders reached out to him to ask if there was anything he could do for Jessie.

Ronnie got into the field because he'd watched his grandmother battle breast cancer on and off for thirty years and eventually have both breasts removed. He was the oldest grandchild, and she had helped to raise him while his parents worked hard to provide for his family. When Ronnie was a teenager, he promised her he was going to make a difference in the fight against cancer, but then she recovered and he quit thinking so much about it. He got married to a great woman, had three children, and worked his way up in a variety of roles in medical diagnostics, but not specifically in the cancer field.

Then his grandmother's cancer returned and spread to her throat. She fought much longer than doctors expected, but eventually it caught up with her at the age of eighty-six. One day before she went to heaven, she reminded him of the promise he'd once made: "Ronnie, you always promised me you'd do something about this, and I don't want you to forget that." He felt ashamed that he hadn't made good on his word. That's when he abruptly switched careers and moved from the world of blood banking to molecular diagnostics, hoping to understand more about individual breast cancers to accelerate the quest to find cures. His mission took him on a circuitous path, and he ultimately took over as top executive at a struggling little company and renamed it Clarient, with the slogan "Taking Cancer Personally."

And while Ronnie was a brilliant businessman, that's not what defined him — he was all heart.

Unbeknownst to me, just before I met Ronnie, he had sold Clarient to GE Healthcare in December in a more than five-hundred-million-dollar deal. In addition to tithing, he and Toni had decided to contribute some of the money toward a children's cancer charity, but they hadn't decided which one yet.

Ronnie and I talked about a lot of things on the day we met — he was the one who educated me about the possibility of a microbiopsy — but when he was done telling me he would do all he could to help Jessie get the right medical treatment, he told me he had prayed about it and decided he also wanted to help Jessie in a different way.

I walked out of his house that day with a check for $10,000 for the foundation, and I barely made it to the car before crying my eyes out. *This is going to mean so much to Jessie*, I thought. I couldn't wait to show it to her. It was the largest donation we'd received by far, and a significant sign that people didn't think of our foundation as just a cute little thing, but as something worthy of that kind of donation. It was a confidence booster knowing that this man trusted us with funding that could have gone to any number of larger organizations.

Jessie was home with Nana, and she jumped up and down when I showed her the donation. She waited by the door for Stacey to come home from work so she could wave the check at her too.

Afterward, Ronnie and Toni invited our whole family over to their house. Jessie was shy at first until their puppy started loving on her, and that broke her shell right open. Soon she was interacting with the Andrews' kids just like they'd been friends forever.

Every couple of weeks after that, they'd invite us over. They wanted to create a safe space for Jessie to hang out where she didn't have to talk about cancer or feel different. Through his work, Ronnie knew that kids with cancer were often sensitive about that—that they just wanted to be like other kids. So while other people were approaching her gingerly with pained expressions and sorrow, he liked to take her out for frozen yogurt in his sports car with the top down. Our family friendship quickly grew very strong. Before long, Jessie was holding their hands and snuggling into them on the couch, just like she did with our own family. That was one of the most special things about Jessie—her ability to show love. Although she was shy with new people, once Jessie loved you, she *loved* you—and you knew it. She would get so excited to see her family and friends, running over to give big hugs and kisses. When Kimmy had come one day to surprise Jessie at school, Jessie ran and leaped into her arms, not caring who saw. She was never embarrassed to show affection in her actions or her words. That's how it became with the Andrews family. She looked forward to those visits greatly and had deep talks with them about her life and goals.

"I see my grandmother's spirit in Jessie," Ronnie told me.

"My grandmother was just like that—always thinking of others before herself. So strong and full of faith."

Ronnie's grandmother hadn't just taken care of her grandkids. She also volunteered to babysit for single moms who couldn't afford to pay regular day-care rates. Although Ronnie's grandmother came from a blue-collar family without much money, they always seemed to have enough. Moms who couldn't afford to pay for babysitting that week were asked to contribute something toward the household, like eggs or milk. That way, all the basic needs were met.

It was a life of service. A beautiful life. All the things that Jesus stood for, Ronnie's grandmother stood for too.

When Ronnie listened to Jessie enthusiastically chat about kids like her chemo buddy Cade or about her JoyJars, he felt like he was seeing his grandmother's heart all over again, and it moved him. He had been focused on breast cancer research and had made amazing strides there, and now that he'd met Jessie and researched cancers like hers, he felt drawn to expand his own focus.

Ronnie taught me things about the cancer world I wish I hadn't known—like the fact that data was out there from other clinical trials that could help Jessie, but those researchers wouldn't share the findings. They all wanted to be the first in the race, the ones to get the Nobel Prize, so they kept anything useful to themselves. In the DIPG world, because it's a rare disease, it takes a very long time for any clinical trial to get a statistically relevant sampling. So it could be several more years before any research breakthrough today would be considered proven enough to be published—and meanwhile, many more kids would die.

"We're going to change people's minds about that," Ronnie

told us. He was a sought-after speaker at medical conventions, and from then on, he preached the importance of sharing research with others instead of hoarding it, and he used Jessie as an example. He told researchers there were children like Jessie whose lives were hanging in the balance and who couldn't afford to wait. Since then, he told me he felt like it was getting through. Maybe that would be another way Jessie could make a difference without even knowing it.

We already knew Jessie was touching people's lives in big ways. We got letters and posts nearly every day from people who said she had inspired them to do something positive. Some messages were from people who also joined the fight against pediatric cancer, and some were from others who were moved to advocate for positive changes in other areas. One young woman even wrote to say she had decided against getting an abortion because Jessie had inspired her to "Never Ever Give Up" — even when a situation seemed impossible. It was stunning to realize there would now be a child in this world who otherwise would not have been if not for the simple actions Jessie took to show her love and spirit.

Some days, Jessie was overwhelmed by the reaction.

"I can't believe all this good stuff that's happening," she told Ronnie.

"I can," he said. "You've inspired a passion in people to go out and make change in the world. Jessie, that's such a good thing. There are people who go through their whole lives and never find that passion, and you've ignited it for a lot of people."

"I don't know how, but I'm glad I did!"

When it came time for our first major fund-raiser, the NEGU Golf Classic, Ronnie and Toni came through for us again, covering the expenses for the tournament so every dollar raised could go directly to the kids. September was off to a terrific start. The golf classic was sold out at 140 golfers and had already attracted some other terrific sponsors too.

Jessie put her own touch on it by insisting there be a fashion show at the end of the tournament—so it was golf followed by dinner and high fashion. She didn't want to be *in* the fashion show; she just wanted to *see* a fashion show, like *Project Runway* in person.

A little weird, but okay, I thought. *Maybe it'll bring out the golfers' wives and girlfriends to join us.* Indeed, two hundred people signed on for the dinner-and-a-show event.

The morning of September 12 was beautiful, and we lined up tables full of JoyJars for all of the participants. Inside the jars were golf balls donated by Wilson, golf shirts donated by Oakley, and various other sponsor-donated items, along with a NEGU wristband. Jessie handed out the jars to many of the golfers herself.

It was thrilling to have her there to cheer everyone on. It was an entirely different mood from the swim-a-thon, when she was suffering from the effects of the radiation and steroids and had to wear a mask. Now she looked and felt much more like herself again, except for the almost nonexistent wisps of hair. At this point, it was almost silly that she bothered trying to hold on to it. There was so little left that it probably would have made more sense to cut it, but she wasn't ready for that. So she wore a baseball cap and her TeamNEGU shirt, and I actually let her drive me around in a golf cart again, even knowing her previous track record. You should have seen her smile.

We had a whole army of volunteers helping out at the event, and free food from Boneheads and Chick-fil-A. The fashion show featured clothing by a local designer, with both models and kids with cancer walking the runway.

The president of UPS's South California district was there because they were sponsoring the event too. Jessie talked to him about her JoyJars, and I pondered out loud, "Wouldn't it be cool if we could get UPS to be the official carriers of JoyJars?" We could save money on postage and keep more money to use for the kids.

Well, because people really *are* good and kind and amazing, that's exactly what happened. One week after the tournament, a UPS representative invited us to her office, where she presented Rick Brotherton and me with a check for $40,000 and offered us a proposal for reduced shipping rates. That, coupled with the money we'd just made from the golf tournament, put the NEGU Foundation in a whole new league. It was no longer a wild dream to think that maybe someday we really could get a JoyJar to every kid fighting cancer, at least in our country.

September was surely our month.

Three days after the tournament, we were getting ready to leave for the tumor microbiopsy at Stanford. The surgeon wanted an updated MRI to see exactly where the tumor was located, so we had scheduled our trip for just after Jessie's checkup. Normally, we left after the MRIs and the results would come by e-mail and phone later in the afternoon, but this time I stuck around and waited so I could make a copy of the results immediately and bring them with us. Stacey took Jessie across the street back to CHOC while I waited for the report. As soon as I had it in my hands, I opened it, trying to make sense of all the usual medical terminology. It's like trying to read a foreign language. But then I got to three words that were as plain as they could be.

A second tumor.

I felt like I had just fallen off a building. Queasy, racing heart, disoriented. A text from Stacey came: "Did you get the report yet? What does it say?"

I managed to walk into the clinic in a panic because I didn't know where Jessie was and I didn't want to run into her before I had an answer. Another doctor who was filling in for Dr. Shen took me and a couple of nurses into her office and opened the report on her computer. I wanted her to tell me I had misunderstood what I'd read. What she told me was worse.

"They see a second growth on the other side of her brain stem," the doctor said.

Everything went dark. I started crying.

It's over, I thought. There wasn't going to be any miracle.

"What's happening?" Stacey texted again. "Do you have the report yet?"

How was I supposed to tell her? How were we supposed to tell Jessie?

"The doctor is looking at it now," I wrote back. I needed time to put myself back together. All I could see were their eyes looking at me, waiting for the news.

Her emotional suffering will be a direct correlation to what she sees when she looks in your eyes.

How was I supposed to look my daughter in the eyes this time, when she was expecting good news? Every report we'd had to this point showed either a reduction in the tumor size or no change, and she had no new symptoms that would have given us a clue that things were going downhill. Even as I prided myself on keeping a realistic attitude and staying ahead of "today," this one still floored me. I thought there would be some clues first, but this time, there were none. Now I was alone with this terrible secret.

I had seen a counselor once a month, and he'd given me some suggestions about honesty and trust with the kids, but there was no role-playing script for this. No counselor can tell a parent how to soften the blow when they've just found out the train is heading for their child.

It was a heavy burden to carry, and I just wanted to set it down, give it to God. *Why, God? Why this girl; why now, why? Why would you do this to a twelve-year-old girl?* And then a more troubling thought crossed my mind—*Are you even real?*

In all the time since I'd given my life to Jesus, I'd never questioned that. But now, just for a brief time, nothing made sense, and I began doubting everything. What kind of an all-powerful, all-loving being would *do* this? Jessie had been doing so well and had so much left to give. Didn't God see her at work in the Joy Factory? Didn't he see her romping with Mr. Moe or playing with her brother or running into Aunt Kimmy's arms? This was a child who was loved and needed here. Why on earth would he need to take her to heaven? What good would it do that would make it worth all the pain?

* * *

"Well, the good news is that your original tumor shrank a little again this month, but there is also some not-so-good news. They found a second tumor on the other side of your brain stem," I told her.

Jessie did not fall apart. She was upset, of course, but she didn't wallow in self-pity. She would talk about how frustrated she felt to have to undergo even more treatments and have more blood work done, but then she'd move on in her mind and look for solutions again.

A friend of mine sent me a YouTube video of the song "One Thing Remains" by Jesus Culture, and Jessie sat on my lap while we watched the lyrics on the screen: *I never, ever have to be afraid. One thing remains. Your love never fails, it never gives up, it never runs out on me.**

It helped both of us to turn again to the simplicity of those lyrics.

"Well, if I have two tumors now, I'm going to need twice as many NEGU Warriors praying for me," Jessie said. She had more than 15,000 Facebook fans, so her new goal was to get to 30,000.

We discussed our options with local doctors and with those doing other trials. Even though the doctor at Stanford was still willing to do the microbiopsy, we decided against it. At this point, we already knew her odds had just fallen even further and that her prognosis was now limited to months. It no longer seemed worthwhile to subject her to another risky procedure. It didn't mean we were willing to accept "there's nothing more we can do," and I guess our doctors realized it by then. Although all along they had told us Jessie had reached her maximum amount of lifetime radiation in that area, suddenly now it was back on the table. They could reirradiate her, they explained—a procedure in which doctors radiate an area that already reached its "full radical dose" previously. It had worked so well the first time in reducing the size of her first tumor, so maybe it would have the same effect on the second tumor and at least prolong her life by a few more months. No one was mentioning the word *cure* even in the "hey, you never know" sense anymore. It was more likely that radiation was back on the table because they didn't expect her to live long enough for the more dangerous

---

*"One Thing Remains," written by Brian Johnson, Jeremy Riddle, and Christa Black Gifford, © 2010 by Bethel Music Publishing (ASCAP)/Mercy Vineyard Publishing (ASCAP)(Admin. by Music Services, Inc.)/Christajoy Music (BMI)(Christa Black is admin. by Bethel Music Publishing). All rights reserved. Used by permission.

effects of radiation to come into play. For instance, while radiation may cause second cancers (like leukemia and breast cancer), those second cancers don't usually crop up for at least five years.

In addition, they offered us a new chemotherapy, Avastin. We discussed it as a family because, at this point, it was as much Jessie's decision as ours. There were no answers. Undergoing radiation (and steroids) again meant another difficult few months ahead as the tumors would swell initially and probably cause all the same symptoms all over again—from weakness and exhaustion to irritability and facial distortion. And although the first chemo wasn't all that terrible on her stomach, this one might be. This second time around could be better or it could be worse, but without it, we knew exactly where the road was headed, and fast. They had already taken her off her current chemo as soon as the second growth was spotted, so we were now in a very anxious space where nothing was being done to combat the tumors. Every moment she was off treatments was a moment the tumors might be growing faster than before.

"God, please help," Jessie prayed with us. "Help us make the right decisions."

We opted to stay close to home at CHOC and try the two weeks of reirradiation and new chemo, which would now be done as an infusion rather than as a liquid she could swallow. Great—more needles. The most I could reasonably hope for now was that she'd live long enough for a second honeymoon period to make the new treatments worth it.

The day before the new radiation treatments would start, Jessie stayed at Nana and Papa's house overnight with Stacey and Kimmy because all the women were going to walk in the Race for a Cure for breast cancer. They participated in this 3.1-mile run/walk every year because Nana was a breast cancer survivor. Each year, Nana would collect another bead for her necklace to show how many years she'd been a survivor.

There was Jessie, with two tumors in her brain, walking to raise money for a "grown-up" cancer. Where were the walks for pediatric cancer? Where was the race for that cure? Seeing the huge strides in breast cancer awareness and funding was inspirational to us because we've seen in our lifetime massive improvements in early detection, survival rates, and treatment options, as well as a new openness in discussing what was once a taboo subject. What they've done is phenomenal, and I don't want to take any of that away from them, but I wanted some of that same awareness shone on DIPG and other cancers that afflict children. It's easy to look at it as just a matter of numbers and statistics—there's more money in curing cancers that affect more people—until it's your child and you're being told that not only is there no cure now, but a cure isn't even on the radar. It's like being told your child is not important enough to save. There are no beaded survivor necklaces for DIPG because there are almost no survivors.

Although she wanted to walk the full course, Jessie had to stop after completing slightly more than a mile. It was cold, and she just didn't have the strength to continue. Miles away at home, neither did I. I had no idea how I was supposed to do normal tasks anymore. Why wasn't the world stopping? My beautiful little girl was not going to be with us much longer, and I was supposed to somehow pretend that anything else mattered.

I didn't pray primarily for healing anymore. I prayed for Jessie to have peace, for a lack of suffering.

By this time, we were using the word *cancer* freely, but we had still never touched on what would happen if the treatments didn't work. I knew it was time to talk about it, but I fell into a very dark rut for a couple of weeks when I didn't do much but watch television. I was curled up in a ball internally, just lost inside, while Stacey stepped up and continued trying to keep things as normal as possible for all three kids—school, homework, movies, swim practice, time with friends. I wasn't sure how she kept it up, but she was a master at the NEGU spirit, even as mine faltered, and she worked on getting me out of my funk.

Once again, we had to take our daughter to have a new mask made to keep her immobilized while they zapped one side of her head with powerful beams. Once again, she would be alone on a radiation table every weekday. And this time, her chemo would be done by injection. There would be more pain and more sickness—and in the end, we had no idea if it would even do anything for her. What do you do with that?

I kept talking to God.

I don't understand you, but I still believe in you. Now you have to be real. I know she is really your daughter and I'm just her earthly dad, but it's very hard for me to understand why you'd need her more in heaven than I need her right here. Why can't you let her be? I know you have the power to do it, so why aren't you healing her? There are so many people praying. She is fighting so hard, and she's one of your servants. I don't want my daughter to go to heaven yet.

I spoke with my counselor about how I was supposed to handle this with Jessie, and his advice boiled down to "be honest." I was gripped with doubts about that, because I knew I hadn't been completely forthcoming about her chances, but now it felt wrong to keep up the facade. I thought about it and thought about it until one Sunday afternoon, Stacey and I sat on the couch with Jessie and Shaya and just said as calmly as possible, "Jess, what do you think about heaven?"

"I don't know ...," she said. "I don't think about it a lot."

"I understand that. But you know we're doing everything we can to fight this, and there's a chance the treatments won't work. Now that there's a second tumor, they can't do the surgery, so we just have to try to trick the tumors now with new medicines."

She nodded.

"St. Jude has been trying to treat this kind of tumor for twenty-seven years, and sometimes it works. There are some kids who have what you have and they've lived a really long time. But there is a chance ..."

How do you say it?

"... that you might go to heaven for God to heal you. It could be like your mission trip, Jess. So we wanted to make sure you know it's the most beautiful place you could ever be. You know it's a place where there's no sickness and no disease, right?"

"Right."

Her lip quivered, then the tears started. Stacey went over and put her arms around Jessie, and Shaya left the room. It felt like pressing on an open wound, but we had to keep going.

"It's not like you see in the movies where you fly around and sleep on clouds. I don't know exactly what it is, but Scripture tells us that God has a room for everyone in heaven."

"But I won't know anyone there."

"Sure you will," Stacey said. "What about Coach Fran?"

Coach Fran was one of her swim coaches who was an award-winning international competitor. He had died a year earlier during a swimming competition in open waters in the United Arab Emirates. It's true that Jessie knew him, but they hadn't been particularly close. It didn't really answer her concern. Her maternal grandparents were still alive—and all of her aunts and uncles and us too.

My father had died of lung cancer and cirrhosis of the liver

a few years earlier, but Jessie and he barely knew each other
—and I didn't suspect my father was in heaven anyway.

"And Kobi and Bruin will be there," I said. They were her
first pets, our two Golden Retrievers that had passed on when
she was about eight years old. Do dogs actually go to heaven?
I don't know, but I didn't care! It was something that could
comfort my daughter, and I went with it. "You're going to get to
take responsibility for them if you get there first. You remember
how Bruin could hold three tennis balls in his mouth? Someone
has to throw those tennis balls to him so he can play the way
he likes."

"Do you really think I'd be in charge of them?"

"Of course you would. They're up there waiting for one of
their family to show up and take care of them, so they'd be right
there on the other side to greet you. They'd belong to you."

Her tears dried up, but not her concerns.

"I'm scared. Coach Fran is the only person I know in heaven."

"Well, there is no fear in heaven, so you don't have to worry
about feeling scared. You won't. And we'll all be there with you
soon. The Bible says it's just a wink. Time doesn't work up in
heaven the way it does down here. Even if it's lots of years down
here on earth, up there it's just a wink until you see all your
loved ones and we're all together again in heaven."

Jessie didn't say much. I knew she was listening, but it was a
lot to take in. Then I called an end to our little meeting so Jessie
could regroup.

"We obviously trust that God's going to take care of everything, but as you know, sometimes kids get to go to heaven
early, so we thought it was important to just talk about it. All
right, let's get ready to go out now."

I don't remember where we were headed after that—
somewhere inconsequential like shopping or another errand.

Normal life stuff, where we'd go stand in line behind strangers who had *not* just discussed death with their children. The weight of our talk hung heavy in my heart for days, but eventually I realized it wouldn't do anyone any good for me to continue sinking into depression.

Instead, I threw myself further into the foundation, one of the few things that still felt meaningful. Ronnie Andrews joined my board of advisers, and his wife, Toni, joined our board of directors. Toni helped me with much of the heavy lifting when it came to seeking out sponsorships, awards, and opportunities for the foundation. She's a tiny Southern dynamo who's not afraid to talk to anyone and tell them exactly why they need to step up and help kids with cancer. Toni had been struggling for some years to find her true passion, and it was a delight to hear that she found it while working alongside Jessie.

We began planning a big gala for January. The gala would be held at a hotel, which Jessie helped me scope out. We decided on the St. Regis Resort and Spa, and we lined up an amazing group of entertainers. Soon after I put out word that I was looking for a headliner, I heard from John Tesh, whom I'd met when he performed at Saddleback.

"I'm all in," he said.

Jessie hadn't seen him perform before, but when I showed her his YouTube videos, she decided his music was cool—and he had "nice hair." He agreed to give a forty-five-minute concert, accompanied by his "Big Band," a seven-piece ensemble. We also lined up jazz musician Tony Guerrero, saxophone and trumpet player Charlie Peterson, and artist Thomas Clark. None of the talents took any payment for their performances.

The gala would be a big formal affair, with awards given out to courageous kids fighting cancer and to kids making a difference by helping our cause in some way—starting "JoyDrives" in their schools or clubs and helping us raise money or awareness.

We decided that since 2012 would be an Olympic year, we'd give the kids gold medals.

"Can I be the one to put the medals around their necks?" Jessie asked.

"I can't imagine anyone else doing it," I said.

I envisioned it as both a fund-raiser for the foundation and a celebration of the people who had helped us get to where we were. Toni spent time interviewing Jessie about her favorite things for a special auction table at the event. We were planning to auction off baskets filled with some of the things she liked best. All of the things Jessie mentioned first were food items—candy, ice cream, red velvet cupcakes, and Aunt Kimmy's famous chocolate chip oatmeal cookies.

"Anything else?" Toni asked.

"I love Harveys bags," Jessie said, referring to a local company that makes bags and accessories out of seat belts.

Jessie wasn't feeling well that day, but she felt at home at the Andrews' house and wanted to participate. She loved sharing her favorite things with people, and her mood brightened the more time she spent with Toni. Yes, "Jessie's Favorites" would be a fun part of the auction, where we'd have more than eighty baskets filled with prizes from hotel stays to spa treatments and sports tickets.

In less than a year, we had made amazing strides and inspired so many people. A big party for all of us would lift our spirits and remind us of the reason we were working so hard to keep growing. Jessie was looking forward to getting dressed up and dancing all night.

I just hoped she would make it there.

decline

Because the tumor and radiation were on the opposite side of Jessie's brain stem this time, her symptoms were likewise reversed. Whereas before, it was the left side of her body that was weakest and "wouldn't listen to her," now it was the right. Her "good" eye now wouldn't close all the way, and she began having pain and fullness in her right ear and numbness in her right cheek.

Radiation made her feel like nails were sticking into her feet and gave her headaches. The nights got tougher. She would often cry out to us in the middle of the night because her legs hurt and she needed us to come in and massage her. For some time, we had a monitor set up in her room so we could always hear when she needed us, but it became easier to just switch places. I slept in Jessie's room, and Jessie slept next to Stacey so someone would always be there with her when she was hurting.

This reminds me to say that my wife, Stacey, is simply amazing. She is so loving, caring, and generous. It's clear to me where Jessie got all of her inner and outer beauty. I could write an entire book on how wonderful Stacey was with Jessie. She clearly could win "Mom of the Year" every year, and especially for the time she spent battling cancer alongside Jessie.

Jessie's new chemo infusions were a long process. She would have to sit in a chair for three hours with a needle in her arm — except for the one time they put the needle in her hand instead. It was supposed to hurt less, but she was in such pain she almost couldn't stand it. Stacey was doing everything she could to help Jessie, but it seemed the pain was not going away.

"I'll call the nurse," I said.

"No, Daddy!" she said, reaching for my arm to hold me back. "I don't want her to think she did something wrong."

"Honey, it's okay. She can just reset it in a different spot."

"No, I'll be fine."

That was Jessie — not wanting others to feel bad even if it meant she would live in pain. I knew Jessie was strong, but told her this was not the time. She vetoed me. We could have helped her, but she chose to wait for the IV bag to stop dripping.

JT and Shaya each wanted to come once to sit with Jessie during chemo. There wasn't much to do but watch movies during the process, considering Jessie couldn't move around. I'm so thankful they both got to come and be with Jessie. They were so encouraging and did everything they could to help her.

Despite her symptoms, she continued making JoyJars and reaching out to people online, and it came back to her in so many loving ways. A young girl wrote a song called "Never Ever Give Up," inspired by Jessie. A woman handmade a doll with a NEGU shirt and donated the money from its sale to the foundation. A family friend bought a JoyJar, filled it with tulips, and brought it to her office to cheer up her coworkers and spread the message.

People wrote to tell her she had inspired them to let go of their arguments and grudges because they realized through her that there were much more important things in life to think about. They wrote to say she had helped them forget about the little stresses in their lives because she put things in perspective for them—she was able to still appreciate everything God had given her despite much bigger challenges than most of them were facing. Her simple and pure faith encouraged many people to connect with God again. People who maybe hadn't prayed in a long time prayed for Jessie, and in doing so, they opened up their hearts to the Lord.

Even though I no longer believed there was a high chance for Jessie to be cured, I still believed in the power of prayer, and we still prayed every day together. When she had to go through her infusions, we'd pray together: *God, like Kari Jobe's song says, you're the healer. You're Jessie's healer, so please help her get through this. Help the needle go in smoothly and help the medicine do its job.*

I quietly prayed for other things too. I prayed the end would not be barbaric, and I prayed she would make it to Christmas. Jessie had asked if we could go to Denver for Christmas.

"You feel up to that trip?" I asked.

"Yeah, let's go visit Kimmy and T and see the snow! It's not a real Christmas without snow."

Stacey and I had agreed to it, and Jessie was so excited. We went there to visit every other year or so to get our fill of "real" winter. The thought of this trip kept Jessie going on days when she got discouraged.

Another major boost for her during that time was to see that her classmates had not forgotten her. We got a call one day from Mrs. James asking if it would be okay if some of the kids came by and played a fun prank on Jessie. We gladly agreed.

One mild weekend evening in October, they made good on that promise. A group of seven boys showed up with Mrs.

James and started toilet-papering Stacey's car. They tossed rolls of toilet paper back and forth over the top of the car until the black car was entirely white. We had been sitting together on the couch watching television when it started. Our dogs barked when they heard noises, so we all ran over to the window and watched what was happening.

"That's the Broskies!"

"The who?"

"That's a group of boys in my school—they call themselves the Broskies. And look! That's Mrs. James!"

It was a delightfully silly moment, watching them try to be quiet and covert while they teamed up to cover the car.

"Hey, I have an idea ... ," Stacey said with a mischievous grin. She pulled out her car keys, which had an alarm button. "Why don't we set off the alarm?"

After much giggling, Jessie decided this was the best idea ever, and she pressed the button. As soon as the alarm sounded, all seven kids panicked and scattered toward the street while we cracked up by the window.

We came out after that and took pictures and thanked them for making our day. Jessie wrote, "It was like for a moment life returned to normal—being with old friends, seeing my teacher, laughing—it just felt so good. Thanks, guys, for stopping by and making me laugh."

Yes, guys, thanks. You have no idea how much we needed to hear that laugh again. Jessie's belly laugh was one of her best features, and it had been a while since we'd heard it. Her energy and mood had been steadily dropping since the second round of treatments had started, and it was great to have people come and lift her up again.

She had finally given in and let one of Stacey's friends cut off her remaining "fringe" hair, and now there was just a bit of stubble coming back in, since the new chemo didn't cause hair loss. Oddly enough, it was coming in dark. We'd heard that hair can change after chemo, but it was still surprising to see blonde Jessie as a potential brunette. JT, in particular, was stumped. "She used to have blonde hair. What happened?" he asked. There was a spot in the back that remained stubbornly bald, though, as a result of where the radiation had hit. Even if she managed to grow her hair out, she would always have a bald patch now. She continued wearing her beanies every day.

At the end of October, I learned from a friend that Eva Longoria was interested in meeting Jessie. Not only did she offer to come out to see us, but she wanted to help Jessie make some JoyJars. I thought it was a great gesture. When the day came, I expected her to arrive with some handlers and a photographer, but I was floored when I saw her come out of her car all by herself, hair slung to the side in a braid and wearing minimal makeup. She had driven all the way from Los Angeles to our house to come and hang out with Jessie and make JoyJars in our garage, with no ulterior motive—just to show support and do something wonderful. I was so unprepared for that kind of casual atmosphere that I merely snapped some pictures and a short video with my cell phone.

As beautiful in person as she is on television, Eva stayed for over an hour and chatted with Jessie, signed things, left her a note on her chalkboard wall, and assembled JoyJars, carefully sticking the labels on perfectly straight and centered. Before she left, she gave me her assistant's phone number and told me to call if we ever needed her.

The next day was Halloween, a holiday that Jessie just loved. Not hard to understand, of course, because of how much she adored sweets. She had gone out trick-or-treating the previous year with her good friend Carly, and the two of them had stayed out until just shy of her nine o'clock curfew. They had walked all over town, eventually running into Shaya and her friends from the swim team. When Jessie got home, she weighed her bag of candy—9.4 pounds. She was ecstatic not only because she had 9.4 pounds of candy, but because it was the first year she beat Shaya.

But this year would be a sharp contrast. Jessie wasn't in any shape to go walking around town, and she wasn't eating anyway, so there was no incentive to go out and beat her record. Instead, she stayed in and helped Stacey and Nana hand out candy to all the kids who came to our door—lots of them—while I took JT out and Shaya went out with her friends. Jessie loved seeing all the little kids in their costumes.

Soon after that day, another troubling new symptom of Jessie's cropped up—dermatillomania, otherwise known as skin picking. She would compulsively pick at her face, causing scabbing all over. We don't know which of her array of medicines was causing this symptom, but she couldn't control it. The open sores were in danger of getting infected, so we tried to solve the problem by putting bandages all over Jessie's fingers, making it difficult for her to "pick." But keeping bandages on every finger for twenty-four hours of each day is a difficult task, so the problem persisted. It became another physical feature that she was embarrassed about, in addition to the hair loss and skinny frame. Her moon face didn't return right away this time; instead, her face thinned out.

Just a few weeks after we met Eva, I did call her assistant again. Jessie seemed to be in a funk and I thought a visit might lift her spirits. Eva arranged for a tour of the *Desperate Housewives* set and an opportunity to meet Marcia Cross. Looking back on the photos of Jessie with Eva each time, it's easy to chronicle her physical decline. In the first pictures, her skin is clear and her face is symmetrical, aside from an ever-so-slight droop on the right side. Just weeks later, her skin is covered in scabs and the right side of her face is paralyzed. Facial paralysis is a common symptom of brain tumors. It meant she could no longer fully smile, but she kept trying anyway. She also didn't have good enough hand coordination anymore to brush her own teeth, so Stacey and I brushed her teeth for her—and she thought it was just *hilarious* to spit out of the side of the mouth she couldn't control anymore so that the water went everywhere.

It became too difficult for Jessie to sit at the computer and type, so for a while we were back to where we were when it all started—Jessie in my lap: "From Daddy's hands and Jessie's heart." But even that started feeling like a chore to her. We told her not to worry about updating her journal so often. She had been writing entries every day until then, along with posting a fun extra poll every few days, which she called "Would You Rather?" It was a series of mostly lighthearted questions about what a person would rather do, given two options: Drink expired milk or eat moldy pizza? Skydive or scuba dive? Swim in a snowsuit or ski in a swimsuit? She loved coming up with the questions—sometimes with the family's help—and reading people's answers. But that ended in October.

The headaches started up again in November. I knew headaches were a bad sign.

Thankfully, she didn't have any on November 19, which was my forty-third birthday. Jessie was in good spirits. When I opened her card to me, it read, "Happy birthday, Daddy. You are the best daddy ever. Thanks for helping me through my treatments. You're the best! XOXO, Jessie."

It was a bittersweet day for me. I was so glad Jessie was happy and able to help me blow out the candles on my cake. She even said, "Make a wish, Daddy." My wish was simple: *God, please heal my daughter.*

We went to Nana and Papa's for Thanksgiving that year, as usual. Nana had several fun traditions we enjoyed, like holiday crackers (also known as poppers), which makes use of an English holiday tradition started in the 1840s by a pastry chef looking for an interesting way to market his bonbons. The crackers are cardboard tubes wrapped in festive paper and twisted on both ends. You need two people to open them—one to pull on each end of the cracker. Then it lets out a "pop" and releases a bunch of prizes inside—a colorful paper crown, candy, a Thanksgiving activity sheet with trivia and puzzles, and a Thanksgiving joke. The kids loved the crackers, and each of us wore our silly paper crowns to the meal that evening.

Each year before we ate dinner, Nana brought out the same cream-colored tablecloth and had each of us trace our hands with permanent marker and then write the year and what we're thankful for. We could write it however we wanted—something we were thankful for in each finger, just one thing right in the middle of the palm, or whatever else we wanted. She'd been doing it since 2003 for the twelve or so of us who sat around her dinner table. There were a lot of handprints on that tablecloth!

Jessie sat between Stacey and me. She asked me to trace her hand for her because her right hand wasn't stable enough to trace reliably anymore. Then she signed her name and wrote the year 2011 and drew a heart inside her handprint, writing next to it in multicolored markers:

I am thankful for ...

> my family
> my doctors
> my friends
> my coaches
> my health
> my teachers

In another spot, she drew lots of hearts and wrote, "I love, love, love Thanksgiving!" We gave thanks for our family, friends, God, and all of our blessings, including the people who were helping us to help others through the foundation. The adults could not write the thing we were most thankful for: *Jessie is still here.* It was a particularly meaningful Thanksgiving because we knew it would most likely be her last.

I hoped Jessie didn't realize that, though. I had recently gone out to lunch with Collie James, whose daughter, Maddie James, also had battled DIPG. Maddie was diagnosed on January 16, 2011, and went to heaven on March 13, 2011 — just shy of two months after her diagnosis. Two months wasn't even enough time to get one's bearings, and yet the family had done so much in that short time. They had made the same two decisions we had early on — that they'd make sure their time with Maddie was lived to its fullest, and they'd do something to properly honor their only child. They also made one decision different from ours. They had thought through that same "Quality" and "Quantity" chart and decided not to pursue treatment. When Maddie was diagnosed, she was already so far along that she was no longer mobile, and there was very little hope for improvement with treatment. They decided it wasn't worth it to make her go through chemo and radiation, knowing she would likely never regain mobility and it wouldn't buy her much time.

I respect that decision and know every family has to make these impossible choices based on their own circumstances and beliefs. I don't think we "did it right." I think we made what we felt was the best decision for our family, and that every other family who has a child with DIPG has the right to choose the course of action they feel is best. Sometimes that means giving up the fight, no matter how much pressure they may get to do otherwise.

Because Maddie so loved sea creatures and had gone to camp at the Ocean Institute in Dana Point, California, her family committed to helping the institute with a special expansion project. They were seeking to raise $1 million to build an educational center for kids like Maddie who wanted to learn about sea life. They accomplished their goal in just three months, and the center was dedicated in her name on what would have been Maddie's sixth birthday. I admired what Collie and his wife were doing, and I looked to him for advice.

I confided I was so worried Jessie would see right through me that she'd look into my eyes and know we had lost all hope of winning this battle.

"What will I do for her when there's nothing left to do? How am I going to look at her in her last moments and help her not be afraid?"

"Erik, you and Stacey will be everything Jessie needs in her last moments, and she will be everything you need."

I clung to those words. They were just what I needed to believe.

My friend Lisa at CBS decided to do a follow-up story about Jessie and the foundation, and this time, they were hoping to tag along as she brought JoyJars to kids. CHOC didn't approve filming at their hospital, but City of Hope Hospital in Los Angeles loved the idea, so we went there. We'd never done that before. The only time Jessie had distributed them herself was at CHOC, and even that was rare. Most of the time the nurses and doctors handed them out, or we shipped them. By then, we had given out 2,500 JoyJars to kids in twenty-seven states.

We piled the jars into Jessie's red wagon, put on surgical masks and gloves, and went from room to room introducing ourselves and handing out the JoyJars. We had to follow a strict routine after every delivery. Between each room, we had to take off our gloves and masks, wash our hands, and put on new gloves and new masks. More than thirty times! Jessie, ever the stickler for rules, was even caught on tape admonishing me: "Wash your hands, Daddy."

Bald kids, kids with tubes and IVs and swollen faces — a floor full of kids who were fighting so hard against what was happening in their own bodies. There was one child in particular who affected us. Her face was covered in tumors, and I could see Jessie's heart break as we left her room. It was a combination of sympathy and fear — *Could this happen to me too?*

The CBS segment aired in November, and it led to a nice bump in traffic to our websites and donations toward JoyJars. Then something even cooler happened. The segment was picked up by many overseas television networks, and Jessie's story became featured in several countries she'd never even visited. A German teen magazine featured her in a double-page center spread! It was a great honor.

Jessie also received the 2012 International Diana Award, established by the British government to honor Diana, Princess of Wales. Jessie's fifth-grade teacher, Mrs. James, nominated her for the award, which recognizes youth in the UK and around the world who are working to make a positive difference and inspire people. Jessie received a certificate signed by the British prime minister, a plaque, and a special pin.

And just as meaningful to us, we got more and more letters from people who were really getting into the NEGU spirit. One family wrote to let us know they had decided not to exchange presents with each other for the holidays that year because they already had everything they needed. Instead, each family member would put the money they would have spent toward filling JoyJars instead.

More than one child even made the decision to "donate a

birthday" to us—asking for donations toward JoyJars instead
of birthday presents. It was so inspiring to Jessie and to all of us.

* * *

We looked for signs of improvement in Jessie's health, but they
weren't forthcoming. December was worse than November. Jessie was becoming quieter and weaker, with less energy to do the
things she loved doing—like writing in her journal and doing
Facebook posts. The last time she wrote in her online journal
was November 7, and it started with this:

> *Hi TeamNEGU,*
>   *What inspires you? My mommy inspires me. She is so*
> *caring, giving 100% every day to me and my bro/sis, she is*
> *a super athlete, very pretty, always makes time for me even*
> *when it's really late and I just want to talk. Best of all ...*
> *her commitment to God inspires me. She has her devotions*
> *every night and I watch her. She is truly my inspiration.*
> *What inspires you?*

After that point, we agreed it was time for her to stop. Stacey
and I continued updating the journal once a week to let people
know what was happening with Jessie, and she just wrote quick
notes on Facebook when she felt up to it. She surpassed 30,000
fans and said her next goal was to get to 50,000—one Like
for every kid in a hospital fighting cancer in the United States.
People helped spread her message far and wide on the Internet in
hopes of helping her achieve her goal. They posted on message
boards, shared her link on Facebook, and made YouTube videos
asking their friends to become fans of Jessie's page. She'd lost
her energy but not her love for the mission.

That month's MRI showed that both tumors were stable,
which didn't explain why Jessie's face was half paralyzed and

why she was suffering from frequent headaches. Doctors had thought those symptoms were from the tumors, but it turned out that there was significant swelling around her cerebellum and frontal lobe and some fluid buildup, which was what was causing the headaches.

To combat the swelling, she went on higher doses of steroids and Diamox, a diuretic used for a variety of conditions ranging from glaucoma to epileptic seizures. Of course, these drugs brought their own cornucopia of unwanted side effects, from more frequent urination to pins-and-needles tingling to the ever-popular irritability. No one is the same on massive doses of steroids. She still had some good days—at least comparatively speaking—but she was not the same anymore.

Once the headaches slowed down, the doctors gave us the okay to taper down on the steroids again, which was a relief. I hoped her mood would improve once the side effects abated. And I knew nothing was a given anymore, but I thought, *Wouldn't it be cool if Jessie made it to Christmas? Please, God? Could you let that happen?*

Jessie never asked for a timetable. I'm sure she had to be worried about her growing symptoms, but she didn't talk about it. She would sometimes bring up heaven in a more casual way, like, "I wonder what kinds of ice cream they have in heaven," or "I wonder what they do for fun in heaven," but she didn't talk about her trip to heaven—except for one day when she called to me from the shower. She was steady enough by then that we didn't need to hold her up in the shower, but one or both of us still stayed in the room with her in case she got dizzy when she tipped her head back to wash her hair and needed a hand to steady her. This time, I was nearby.

"Daddy? If I go to heaven—like when I'm thirteen or fourteen—it's just a wink, right?"

"Yes, honey, it's just a wink."

"Okay."

I was glad for the steam in the bathroom as it masked the tears streaming down my face.

Dear Lord, don't let her leave me. I'm not ready for this.

christmas

A few weeks before Christmas, Jessie had a major breakthrough — she ate.

It wasn't exactly a turkey dinner with all the trimmings, but it was something. Oatmeal, to be precise. Just a little more texture than her usual smoothies and shakes. She did it because she knew Christmas was coming and wanted to be able to eat when she got to Kimmy and T's house. There were certain specialty foods she loved to eat in Denver that she never got to eat elsewhere, like at a restaurant called Noodles & Company, which we don't have near us. Eating again wasn't something we talked her into. She just decided she wanted to try something that morning, and she did it. She was so excited about that oatmeal that we took a picture of it, and then she called Kimmy at work.

"I ate!" she said.

"You did?"

It was a huge deal. Everyone at Kimmy's work knew what was going on, and they danced with her in celebration. Jessie had been on a liquid diet for four months, and that morning, she broke through the barrier that had been holding her back. Once she was past it, you'd be amazed at how that little girl could power down food. We loved every moment of it and regularly took pictures of her eating again. The little everyday things that other people would never think of as momentous were prime photo moments for us: *Look, that's Jessie eating a sandwich! Look, here she's eating spaghetti!* Now the challenge would be to make sure she continued eating relatively healthy foods instead of devouring the four months' worth of candy she had been missing.

Doctors were nervous about Jessie flying in her condition. Because of the swelling, she went for another MRI and found little improvement, even though the headaches had lessened somewhat. They told us to take oxygen tanks with us because of the higher altitude in Denver and prescribed extra pain medication in case things got worse while we were away. The high altitude could lead to increased cranial pressure. Just before we left for the trip, Jaime met Jessie in the chemo room to give her a present—a Build-A-Bear stuffed animal to take with her on the plane.

What fun would a trip be without a little last-minute panic, though? We rented a travel-size oxygen machine that we were told would be no problem to take on the flight, but when we got there, the airline wouldn't let us take it with us. Gate attendants told us we needed clearance for the oxygen tanks forty-eight hours in advance of a flight and said we had to leave them behind. No amount of "but my daughter has cancer!" would sway them, so we had to order an oxygen machine to be delivered to T and Kimmy's house.

That left the question of what to do with the rented oxygen machine we were currently holding. We surely didn't want to leave it at the gate, so I called Tanta and she rushed over to the airport to meet me at the curb to grab it and deliver it back to the medical supply company. Like in any good movie scene, we ran right down to the wire, and the kids were worried I wasn't going to make it back in time to board the plane. But I did.

We got to Denver the week before Christmas, with special permission from Saddleback for me to miss the Christmas Eve services for the first time in fourteen years. I was very grateful that Pastor Rick understood our need to be with family and to make Jessie's wish come true.

At that point, Jessie's hair had grown past the stubble stage and was now short and brown. It was a relief that she didn't feel the need to wear beanies every day anymore and was less self-conscious about it. However, there were other things to be self-conscious about now, such as the fact that she'd lost all hearing in one ear. We originally assumed it would come back once the effects of radiation wore off but were dismayed to learn we were wrong. Dr. Shen told us this would be a permanent side effect. Our little girl was now essentially blind in one eye and deaf in one ear, and we had to put bandages on her face some days when the skin picking had gone too far.

When someone is so limited, I think it's natural to turn inward. That's what was happening with Jessie. She withdrew in ways she never had before. Whereas she had been looking for-ward to the snow before, now she sat on the couch and listened to audiobooks on her iPad or played games by herself while Shaya and JT ran around outside without her. Once, I got her to go outside long enough to pull her around on a sled for a few minutes. Aside from that, she didn't venture out of the house except when we went out with the family to eat or shop.

The women all went to high tea at a historical hotel down-town, and they went shopping and to Cinnabon a couple of times. Luckily, Jessie was eating pretty normally now and w able to enjoy the meals, especially at Noodles & Company. The women also cooked a traditional Norwegian meal at home. There were a couple of tense moments when everyone stared at Jessie because we were worried she was about to choke, but they were false alarms.

Christmas morning should have been the high point of our trip, but it started out as one of the worst days we'd ever had.

Jessie woke up at about 2:00 a.m. and crawled into our bedroom, crying out in severe pain. This time, it was something new—knee pain. We tried calming her down and getting her back to sleep, but that didn't work. We massaged her legs for more than two hours and gave her pain medication, but the pain wouldn't let up. It was the worst pain we'd ever seen her in.

"What can I do?" Jessie asked in desperation.

Stacey texted the case manager. I don't know why she was awake at that hour, but she texted her right back.

"You have the comfort kit from Dr. Shen's traveling nurses," she wrote. "The kit has morphine in it. It's time to use it."

But we didn't want it to be "time to use it." Morphine was a big step—and not one we wanted to take with our daughter on Christmas morning in Colorado. It wasn't one I wanted to take *anywhere* at *any time*, but especially not here.

"Are you sure you need it, Jess?" Stacey asked her. "Morphine is some pretty serious stuff. You don't want to take it unless you really need it."

Stacey now says she wishes she hadn't given Jessie a hard time about it, but we both felt like it was crossing a new threshold that meant things were really bad—and we didn't want to acknowledge things were that bad. But we had no other choice. We gave her the morphine and watched as Jessie finally relaxed and got loopy. The pain faded. We were the only ones awake now, and in a couple of hours, the whole family would gather around the tree for the happiest and holiest day of the year. What would it be like?

Jessie awoke in better shape, though we had to continue giving her morphine throughout the day. She took her position as the gift coordinator, handing out presents to everyone and watching the reactions. She'd made personalized Shrinky Dink ornaments for each person, along with buying stocking stuffer gifts and helping to wrap everything.

One of the things she'd asked for that year was an iGuy—a funny-looking, squishy foam cover for her iPad that could stand on its legs. Jessie knew we hadn't been able to find it locally, but Kimmy found one for her, making it one of the best surprises of the day. She gasped with excitement.

That was the thing about Jessie—you wouldn't have known what kind of night she'd just had. She bounced back so readily, never dwelling on the things that brought her down.

I thought, *Maybe it was just all the walking.* We had gone walking around the mall on Christmas Eve, and I hoped the knee pain was just a temporary result of that. We stayed until December 30, and although she had trouble sleeping some nights, the pain didn't get that extreme again.

One night, Kim made her famous chocolate chip oatmeal cookies, which the kids call "Kimmy Cookies," and Jessie was very chatty as she ate them by the handful.

"Your cookies are the best. They're even better than Mommy's cookies."

"Uh, thanks. I'm sitting right here, you know," Stacey said.

"Sorry, Mommy!" Jessie laughed. Then she told Kimmy all about the cookie exchange Stacey had done the previous year with the coaches at the pool.

"After we get home, we're going to have this cookie exchang

and all the coaches will come over and we get to try out all the different kinds of cookies that everyone makes. It's so great!"

Stacey glanced over at Kimmy—she hadn't planned any such thing that year because we had so much going on, and besides, now it was after Christmas. But of course, now that Stacey heard how much Jessie was looking forward to it, she decided she'd start planning a cookie exchange for January. Anything that drummed up that much enthusiasm from Jessie was worth doing. Jessie seemed to end the vacation stronger than she started it, and we became hopeful.

She made it through Christmas. Wouldn't it be awesome if she made it to her thirteenth birthday?

Jessie had been diagnosed on March 3, 2011. April 8, 2012, would be just over thirteen months from then—well within the twelve-to-eighteen-month time span the doctors had predicted she could live. If we could just get past the swelling, she'd feel better. There were so many kids looking up to her and benefiting from what she had created. I wanted her to see more of her efforts paying off. We had just made it to three thousand JoyJars delivered—amazing for a period of just eight months, but there was still a long way to go.

We arrived home from Colorado to find that our house had been Joy Mobbed. Our front door was covered by a giant heart made up of hundreds of little blue NEGU signs. What a loving homecoming! Jessie couldn't wait to greet Mr. Moe. She'd had a hard time leaving him behind.

The day after we returned, Stacey went to get a tattoo. Stacey and her friend Rachele at work had batted around the idea several times, but they hadn't made a move until Rachele texted Stacey, while we were in Denver, to say that her daughter Paige wanted a tattoo as well.

"We should all do it together and get those tattoos we've always talked about," Rachele wrote.

"Okay, make the appointment," Stacey answered.

"Really?"

So Rachele called White Lotus and made an appointment with Greg Pugh for the three of them, mentioning that she wanted to get "Never Ever Give Up" tattooed on the side of her foot.

When Greg got home, he said to his wife, Kat, "I'm doing a special tattoo tomorrow. Someone is coming in to get a 'Never Ever Give Up' tattoo. Isn't that the NEGU thing that little girl Jessie started?"

She said yes. His wife had been talking about us since finding Jessie's page online.

"I'm going to get Jessie to do a NEGU tattoo on me," he told her.

"Don't get your hopes up. It's probably not her family."

But, of course, it was. You could never really plan things with Jessie in advance because her condition changed so much from day to day, so Stacey hadn't mentioned the tattoo appointment until that morning—New Year's Eve. It seemed Jessie was in good shape, so Stacey told her about it and asked, "Wanna come with?"

"Sure!" Jessie said.

When they got to the shop, Greg took one look at Jessie and said, "Did you know you're a rock star?" He got her laughing right away.

Stacey got a tattoo of three Hawaiian flowers with the birthstone colors of each of our kids in the middle and the words "Never Ever Give Up" on her ankle, followed by "Phil. 4:13." Rachele and Paige both got "Never Ever Give Up" tattoos too. The women had no idea going into it how long the proces would take—all in all, it took five hours. It was a good thing they didn't realize that in advance, because Stacey never would have asked Jessie to come along. Five hours was an extremely long day for Jess, and there was no way to predict if she'd stay in good condition all that time. But luckily, it was a really good day, and her spirits were high. Jessie took pictures and laughed at all the faces the women made when the needle burned or pinched.

Greg and Jessie chatted so much throughout the time that she forgot to eat her lunch. Her meatball sub sat under her chair until it got cold. And just as he'd envisioned, Greg asked Jessie if she'd tattoo the word "NEGU" on his hand.

"Me? But ... I don't know how to tattoo!" she said.

"That's okay. I'll talk you through it."

She laughed and agreed, and he showed her how to draw the word in ink first, then put on gloves and use the tattooing needle to fill it in with ink.

With hand-steadying assistance from Osh, one of the workers at the tattoo shop, Jessie neatly wrote the letters N-E-G-U and then she wrote two dots. Greg was perplexed, wondering what was with the dots, and then, as he says, "She did something more innocent and perfect than I'd ever seen. She made a mouth under the two dots because she was drawing a smiley face. It is what I have described since then as a divine moment in my life. At that very moment, I saw pure innocence, kindness, selflessness, and love all in one little gesture. I have never experienced anything like it in my life."

Jessie changed Greg's life that day. He's told me himself, and so has his wife. They both say that his entire demeanor changed the day he met Jessie. He was able to control the anger he had struggled with and became a more caring, positive person.

Afterward, he offered to do NEGU tattoos for just $20 for

anyone who wanted them, and he would donate the entire $20 to the foundation. He would draw the tattoo any way the client wanted, except he wouldn't copy the tattoo Jessie gave him—that was too special to him to share with anyone else.

It was a beautiful gesture and showed me that you can always use your talents for good causes. Some people have bake sales to support their favorite causes; Greg donated his tattooing skills.

I believe each one of us has talents and skills we can use to do good in the world, and it's just a matter of thinking creatively about how to best make it work. If you've thought about helping a charity but don't know where to start, the answer might be as simple as what you're already doing—just directed differently.

Maybe you have a business you can use to support a cause you care about, but if not, think about the other things you do have. Can you knit? Then knit warm hats and gloves for people in shelters near you. Are you a good musician? Offer free lessons to kids in disadvantaged areas. Are you a good writer? Offer to write articles or press releases for your favorite local charity. Are you good at talking to people? Offer to head up a fund-raising committee for an animal rescue group.

Taking the first step is the hardest part. It's all about breaking new ground in your mind. But once you start, you begin to see that this is the only way anything good ever gets done. It's not "other people" who are responsible for making our world a better place; *it's us.* We get to take care of each other. Jessie figured that out early in life, but it took me—and a lot of other people—much longer to find where we're called to be.

Greg and his wife became actively involved with our work, and soon they were expecting a little girl of their own.

I think Jessie was exactly where God intended her to be that day.

the final day

I want you to picture Jessie giving Greg that tattoo on New Year's Eve, posing for pictures with him afterward, smiling as hard as she could—even though the right side of her face was paralyzed—because less than a week later, she would never smile again.

As we headed into the new year, she wrote a note to her Facebook fans:

> Have a NEGU New Year! Thank you SO MUCH for
> supporting me the last nine months as I have fought my two
> brain tumors. Your prayers and posts keep me going when
> I get tired, so please keep praying and posting. We still pray
> for God to heal me each day. He loves all of us so much.
> I just know 2012 is going to be a much better year =).
> XOXO, Jessie

Three days later, she went for her next chemo infusion, and she asked people to send her NEGU videos to watch to keep her spirits up while she was in the hospital. Bart Millard, the le singer of MercyMe, e-mailed her a video of his family in their car saying, "We NEGU ... do you?" She loved it.

But her headaches had returned, and she was feeling very sleepy and not "with it." New Year's Eve had been her last good day. Her answers to questions got shorter. She didn't volunteer conversation much anymore except when people directly engaged her. Such was the case when Ronnie put his arm around her and spoke with her one afternoon.

"So the gala is coming up in just a couple of weeks. What do you want me to think about as we head there?" he asked her.

"Mr. Andrews, I just want to raise enough money so that every kid who is told they have cancer will get a JoyJar this year."

Is that all? he thought. Some quick calculations told him that, at $20 per jar, that was a cost of about $1 million to cover all the kids fighting cancer in hospitals in the United States.

"Well, Jessie, that's a mighty big goal, but let's pray about it," he said. They held hands. "God, this is a big request, but you're bigger than all that. Help us figure out a way to make it happen."

Ronnie knew an awful lot about cancer, and just like me, he had studied the signs of the end stages. We both knew what the end was going to look like, with the weeks of organ failure breaking her down until she was unable to move or eat and probably unable to speak.

I continued to reach out to other parents whose children had recently lost their fight with DIPG, trying to get some glimmer of hope and help. I just didn't want to see my sweet pea's life slowly taken away from her day after day. Some parents told me they just would hold nightly prayer vigils around their kids. Others gave me vivid details of their child's last days. Nothing was really helping, except to have all of them tell me that the medicine really does make them look peaceful. I didn't want my daughter to *look* peaceful if she was mentally aware her body was shutting down. That sounded like hell to me.

But what everyone had described to me was not what happened to us at all.

"Erik! Erik! I can't wake Jessie. Something's wrong."

It was 4:30 a.m. on January 5, 2012. I was upstairs sleeping in Jessie's bed, and Stacey had been downstairs with Jessie. Normally, they slept in our room, but Jessie had fallen asleep on the couch that day while Nana was babysitting, and Stacey didn't have the heart to wake her to move her.

January 4 had been a difficult day for Jessie. She'd had a terrible headache that wouldn't abate and was on morphine every three hours. She slept a lot that day, and we were supposed to take her in for a CT scan the following morning to figure out where the pressure was coming from. Stacey slept on the other end of the L-shaped couch, waking Jessie every three hours for her medicine. Jessie vomited up the medicine once that night and kept apologizing for vomiting—and that broke Stacey's heart.

"Honey, it's not your fault," she said. "Please don't worry about it."

They both fell back asleep, but when it was time to administer the next dose of morphine, Stacey couldn't get Jessie to respond. Her body was rather limp and she wasn't very conscious.

I flew down the stairs and into the family room, where I immediately heard the sound—rattling. Her breathing was labored in a way that told me this could be it. As a pastor, I've sat with many families in the last hours, and this sound was common to all of them. My heart sank as I stared at my little girl.

"Jess? Jessie, can you hear me? We have medicine for you, but we need you to wake up. Can you hear me? Please open your eyes, Jess."

There was little response other than the terrible noise of her struggle to breathe. The words caught in my throat. "Stace, this is bad. This could be it."

"But this isn't right ..."

We hadn't had our warning. We were supposed to know when the end was coming so we could be more prepared than this. I was terrified and confused and just wanted my daughter to breathe normally.

Please, God, don't let her suffer.

Stacey and I discussed calling 911 but decided against it because we didn't want people who'd never met her to come in and take over. I called the hospice team, and they had Gay Walker call me right back. Gay was the woman I had met with when she first came in for an interview at my office.

"What's going on? What are her symptoms?" Gay asked.

"She's not really responding to us. We can't get her to open her eyes much. Her breathing is labored," I said. "It sounds terrible."

"Is she lying on her back?"

"Yes."

"Okay, I want you to roll her over to her side. That's her epiglottis causing the sound you're hearing, and it'll get better if she's on her side. Then I want you to get her oxygen machine and get that started right away."

Getting her onto her side did help somewhat, but I couldn't get the oxygen machine to work. Stupid machine! Stacey was on the phone trying to get information from the nurses as I grew ever more frustrated with the oxygen machine. Then I called Gay back.

"I'm heading out the door now, so I'll be with you as soon as I can. It will take me about forty minutes to get there. But, Mr. Rees, it sounds like Jessie might go to heaven today. This is how it goes. You might want to call the people you want to be around her."

I told Stacey, and the two of us broke down. It was the worst news I could imagine telling our family, but we had to do it. I quickly called Stacey's parents, Kimmy and T, and Tanta and Bob.

"Something happened to Jessie in the middle of the night, and she's not responding," I said. "The hospice team is on its way, and they're suggesting we gather our family."

Kimmy and T packed their bags and headed straight for the airport. Nana and Papa and Tanta and Bob got into their cars.

Gay arrived first and headed straight in to examine Jessie, picking her up to a sitting position. Jessie's head wobbled involuntarily.

"Jessie, it's your nurse, Gay, and I'm going to give you some morphine to help you feel better."

As it turned out, Gay was exactly who we needed at that moment. She changed the atmosphere from panic to order, reminding us of all the things that still made sense.

"Let's put on some of Jessie's favorite music," she said, and we did. "She can hear you. Go ahead and talk to her."

We held her hands and said, "Hey, honey. We love you. We're here."

With her eyes just half open, she mumbled, "Love you."

The words weren't articulated, but they were clear. They were the last words Jessie would speak.

Another nurse named Lisa arrived. Jessie had been having mild seizures, so the nurses gave her medications intended to calm her body down. At about seven o'clock, I said, "We have to wake the kids. What should we tell them?"

"Kids do better with reality than imagination," Gay suggested. She gave us her thoughts on what to say, and we ended following them. Stacey and I headed to Shaya's room first. I knelt next to the bed, and Stacey sat at the foot of the bed. It wasn't normal for both of us to come in to wake her like this, which had to be the first sign for her that something was going on.

"Honey, something happened last night to Jess. There are nurses here, and Jessie is okay—she isn't in any pain—but she has oxygen going into her nose and she's on pain medications. They think she might go to heaven today."

Shaya started crying. Stacey held on to her.

"You can come down and see Jessie now if you want, or you can stay here and wait a little while. Are you okay?"

She was not okay. She just kept crying. We left to check on Jessie, and, in retrospect, we probably should have stayed with Shaya a little longer. Decision making isn't at its finest when you're in shock. All I could think about was Jessie's seizures and whether or not they'd stopped. We got back downstairs and found her in the middle of another seizure.

"Erik, what's happening?" Stacey asked.

I lit into one of the nurses. "Make this stop *now*. I was told she wasn't going to suffer!"

They administered more and more medication until, finally, Jessie's body quieted down. This was what palliative care was all about. Here we were, all too soon, arriving at the moment doctors had warned me about from the very start.

We went back upstairs to wake JT, and Shaya joined us in his room. Just as we'd tried so hard to mask our emotions all along to avoid scaring the kids, now it was Shaya who worked so hard to pull herself together for the sake of her brother. The three of us surrounded him as we told him the same things we'd told Shaya. He cried.

Shaya put her hands on his shoulders and looked him right in the eyes and said, "I love you, JT, and we're going to be okay."

She comforted him in ways that we couldn't. When they finally went down to see Jessie, I could see how uncomfortable JT was. They both told Jessie that they loved her, and then JT stood around awkwardly. He said, "I wonder if there are any cartoons on," and we told him to go ahead and check. Shaya went with him, watching over her little brother. I wondered if we had done the right thing by not preparing them for this moment. Some things can be answered only in hindsight.

Stacey never again moved from Jessie's side. She just sat and held her hand. When Nana, Papa, Tanta, and Bob came, they each sat with Jessie, stroking her hair and talking to her. I paced. I sent out a post on Facebook asking people to pray for Jessie's comfort.

"Why don't we let Mr. Moe come in and sniff her?" Gay suggested. We did, and then we put him and our other dogs in the office to lessen the confusion. I didn't know what to do with myself, and I wasn't sure how I wanted things to go that day. Would it be right if everyone was in the room with Jessie when she took her last breath? Should it be just Stacey and me?

Kimmy and T's flight was delayed. They had to sit on the tarmac for fifteen minutes before they could disembark. When they arrived in the terminal, they gave up on waiting for their luggage and just left without anything, figuring they could come back for it later. It was more important to get to us.

By eleven o'clock, I saw that Jessie's hands and feet were turning light blue. I knew that the body changes colors from the limbs inward toward the core as the blood stops circulating. From the look on Gay's face, I realized she had seen it too. Jessie was getting ready to join Jesus. I kept checking my watch and waiting for the door to open. We were in a race against time now, and I knew how much it would hurt Kimmy in particula if she didn't get to see Jessie before she passed. We knew th plane had touched down because they'd called. All we could say was, "Get here." Now we couldn't get through.

So we talked to Jessie. "Hang in there, Jess. Kimmy and T are on their way to see you right now. They'll be here any minute. They can't wait to see you. They love you so much, Jess."

Jessie's breaths were slower now, with long pauses. I brokenly prayed, "God, I surrender Jessie to your loving hands. She is your daughter. Thank you for allowing me to be her daddy. Please save her from pain and help us walk each day with her in our hearts."

At twelve minutes past eleven, Jessie was in Stacey's arms, and her hands were blue. She took a breath and then—silence. I watched as the nurses checked her pulse and blood pressure. Then, as more of a statement than a question, I said, "She's gone."

"Yes," Gay said softly. "Jessie is no longer with us."

The oxygen machine was turned off. There was nothing but silence and the sound of crying reverberating through the house.

At 11:20, the front door flew open. Kimmy came rushing around the corner and looked right at me. *Did I make it?* her eyes seemed to ask.

I shook my head.

The sound of her wailing pierced my heart as she ran to Jessie and collapsed by her side.

For the next half hour, all we did was cry. Then Gay said, "There's no timetable for this, but let me tell you what has to happen next. We'll need to call the mortuary to have Jessie picked up. I need your permission to get her changed into some cleaner clothes."

Dying is not a neat or sterile process. All the women—Stacey, Kimmy, Tanta, and Nana—helped to get Jessie dressed. They kept her draped in a sheet to preserve her dignity while they did

I can't imagine what that experience was like for them, but it was somehow soothing to me to know that the most significant women in her life were helping Jessie with such compassion one last time.

Tim had gone upstairs to be with Shaya and JT, and he came down with them so they could be with Jessie before she would be taken away. JT just stood and stared at her and cried.

"It's okay, buddy," I told him. "She's cancer-free now. She's in heaven, and she's all healed."

It is what I believed, but that didn't make it easier for either one of us. Eventually I pulled Stacey aside and asked, "How long do you want her to be in the house?" It was no longer our daughter—only our daughter's body. We agreed it was time to call the mortuary.

Liz, the woman from our church who handled all the memorial services, came over to talk to us, and at about one o'clock, the men from the morgue arrived. "We're so sorry for your loss, Mr. and Mrs. Rees," they told us. They had a gurney with them and motioned to it. "Is it okay to proceed?" they asked.

At that point, I cleared out the room, except for Stacey and me, because I just couldn't stand the thought of people watching Jessie's body being placed on and carried out on the gurney. Jessie was wrapped in a quilt made for her by her teammates. The men lifted her onto the gurney, and we kissed her forehead.

"Would you like us to cover her face with the sheet?" one of the morticians asked.

"Please, no," I said.

I asked them to pull the van as close to the garage as they could, again to lessen the spectacle of carrying her out. We followed behind them out through the garage, and as we reached the garage door, I could see everyone watching and crying from the windows. I said, "You can cover her face now."

The morticians drove away, and I just sat down where I

in the driveway and cried. People came out and touched my shoulder and tried to bring me back inside, but I refused. "I just want to be alone, thank you," I said. I sat there for quite some time, just reliving everything in my mind, wondering what I could have done better. You question everything when there are no answers.

Did I do all right? I didn't know if I was everything she needed in those last moments, but she was everything I needed.

When I did get back inside, there were conversations happening all around me.

She was so strong at Christmas.

How could this happen so soon?

When I could see through the tears again, I consulted Stacey about what to say and then sat down on the computer chair where Jessie had so often sat on my lap and composed the message I had long dreaded writing.

Dear friends,

We have prayed and prayed and prayed for sweet Jessie to be healed here on earth, but God's plan was to use heaven for healing. Jessie earned her wings today and is with Jesus now!!! No pain ... complete vision ... spreading joy.

Please pray for our family as we walk out of the valley of death and toward the mountaintop. We will let everyone know of her celebration service as arrangements are made. Please join us in carrying on her joyful spirit and Never Ever Give Up attitude.

Much love,

Erik, Stacey, Shaya, and JT

The next day was full of tears. I went to Jessie's room and smelled her clothes, lay down in her bed, cuddled up with Moe the floor, tried to feel her presence. That day, like every day that would come after it, I relived those last six hours of her life from the moment Stacey woke me to the moment they took Jessie away on a gurney. How do you process that? I hadn't even started.

That day is a fog. I remember our friends David and Jenny showing up with coffee for us that morning, and I remember that Kimmy slept over. We looked at a lot of pictures of Jessie and our family. And on that day, Jessie reached her milestone from heaven—50,000 fans. One for every kid fighting cancer in a hospital.

You did it, sweet pea.

If I had thought Jessie's passing was going to give me any answers, it didn't. I accepted that this was God's will, but I sure didn't like it. Somehow the world was still turning all around me. Why was the world still turning? It was supposed to stop! My child was gone.

My attention had been focused on Jessie's well-being for the last ten months and two days, and now it was time to focus on the rest of my family. I wanted so much to make sure they were all okay, but, of course, none of us were.

We didn't have a viewing, but Kimmy went to see Jessie's body in the morgue to try to get some sense of closure. "She looks so peaceful," she told us. I just didn't want my last memory of my daughter to be in a morgue. My daughter wasn't in that morgue; she was in heaven. And I felt so empty.

We had to decide that day about what would happen to Jessie's body. We didn't have a family plot at a cemetery, so where would she be buried? We were talking about places, thinking about what would happen if we moved and couldn't visit Jessie's grave site regularly, so we talked through the idea of cremation and placing her remains in a vault. The next day, we visited cemetery and picked out a spot and paid for it, but then th called us later to tell us the urn we had chosen wouldn't fit in that spot, so what did we want to do—change the urn or change the spot? That's when Shaya spoke up.

"Why are we putting Jessie in a cemetery next to some strangers? That's not what she would want. She wouldn't want to be surrounded by people she doesn't know. She'd want to be here with us."

And so it was that we made the decision to have Jessie's body cremated and to bring her urn home with us.

When it arrived, covered in velvet, we placed it on a shelf. It was a simple white marble rectangular urn. JT looked at it for a minute, then disappeared into the living room. We assumed he was just feeling uncomfortable, so we gave him some space. But when he came back, he was carrying a folded 3 x 5 index card on which he had written "Jessica Joy Rees"—like a little place card. He placed it next to the urn.

"Mommy, if that's Jessie in there, then everybody should know who she is," he said.

We've never moved that index card. Everybody *should* know.

a celebration of life

When we opened our door to head to Jessie's Celebration of Life service on January 11, we found an astonishing sight. Trees all the way from our door as far as we could see were covered with blue and turquoise ribbons and balloons (the NEGU colors) and posters with messages like "Jessie will be missed," "Gone but not forgotten," "Our little angel," and "We'll NEGU for Jessie." Each class at her school had made a poster of a JoyJar, and individual students, teachers, and parents made dozens of other signs.

We didn't know how far the decorations went until we got in the car and drove. They went all the way from our door to the church, about two miles. Someone had even pressed blue tissue paper into a NEGU collage on the fence above a road barrier. There were blue ribbons around stop signs and traffic light poles. The Melinda Heights Elementary School's mural in front of the building featuring their mascot—a mountain lion —now had the word "NEGU" added in a speech bubble. One big tree at an intersection had blue ribbons tied to every branc —more than one hundred ribbons.

It gave me chills. People who'd never even met Jessie had risen hours early that morning to ensure that our entire path to the service would be a visual reminder that the community was mourning with us. We felt important and special that day. For a little while, the world *did* stop for us.

See, Jess? Look at what you meant to people, I thought. This is how I would communicate with my daughter from now on … I couldn't speak to her in person anymore, but that didn't mean the conversation ended. I spoke to her all the time in my thoughts and prayers.

In the days after Jessie's passing, we received an astonishing number of letters and cards telling us how Jessie had affected people. I read them all, and they gave me comfort. Here are a few samples:

> Dear Jessie,
>
> I write this letter directly to you because I don't want to write this as if you are not here — you are now here with us in spirit. Words cannot describe how deeply saddened I am that you have left us so soon. I heard about your diagnosis around nine or ten months ago through a family friend who posted on Facebook to "pray for this little girl." Since then, I have been following your story, praying for you and your family, reading your journal, paying attention to your Facebook posts — being there for you since the beginning of your journey. As I continued to be your support via the Internet, I felt I needed to do more for you, so I signed up to be a volunteer for NEGU. I felt like you have done so much for me and others, and it was time for me to help you fulfill your dream.
>
> It's amazing how I feel like I know you, feeling such a bond to you and your family. I feel as if I lost someone dear to me. But in this short time that I got to know you, you really have

changed me, helping me become a better person. You have inspired me to continue to push, fight, never ever give up. You remind me what it is like to be selfless, what it is like to help others, what it is like to be a fighter.

I grow out my hair and donate it every two or three years in memory of my little cousin who passed away (Meghan Flynn, '98 – '04) from leukemia. But I thought this year it was your turn. I wanted to honor you for being so courageous! So last week I cut 13" because you were turning 13 this year! I had read your post that morning (1/4) about how your headaches were so painful. I said a prayer and thought to myself, "This will cheer sweet lil' Jessie today." I mailed my hair the day before you passed in your honor (to Wigs for Kids). Now it is in your memory.

I never got the chance to meet you here on earth, nor to express my gratitude to you. But I need to tell you thank you. This whole time you have been thanking everyone for their help and support, but we need to also thank you for doing the same for us. Thank you for allowing us to enter your life and get to know you. Thank you for educating us and bringing awareness to pediatric cancer. Thank you for giving hope to all those children fighting for their lives. Thank you for teaching us life lessons of what it really means to be courageous. Thank you for showing us how to make the best of a situation. Thank you for spreading the love and JOY that you represent. Thank you for reminding us to have faith. But most importantly, thank you for inspiring us all to NEVER EVER GIVE UP. You are the symbol of what it means to NEGU.

Your little body may have given up, but your soul never ever gave up ... I cannot wait to meet you in heaven and give you a hug!

XOXO — Julia Fernandez

Hi Erik,

I learned about Jessie and her condition pretty soon after her diagnosis through a friend on Facebook. I daily looked forward to reading her upbeat, hopeful, and sweetly stated status updates. Like so many others, I shared her story with my own friends and then sat back and watched as TeamNEGU took off like wildfire with Jessie's sweet spirit as the driving force behind it all. I prayed for her daily, and as I cried like a baby while watching her news interview, I felt even more led to pray for her. Even when she started posting about those darn headaches, I just believed the Lord was going to heal her. Then, a couple days later, a random Facebook check proved he had other plans. I'll never forget standing in the middle of my bedroom, cell phone in hand, unable to move because of what I read and then reread what must have been ten times. How could it be? My finite little mind could not wrap itself around the fact that she was gone. I cried all the way to work … for someone I had never even met.

Who Jessie was and what she did touched my heart in a very real and profound way. I became a single mom two years ago after leaving an abusive marriage. I'm back at work full-time, and my life is hectic, busy, and pretty whirlwind-ish. I want you to know that the Lord used your precious little girl mightily to encourage me over these months and also to remind me that I CAN do all things through Christ, who gives me strength! If Jessie could, simultaneously, courageously fight cancer AND be an encourager to thousands of people across the world, then I could surely keep my head up and stay strong in my own battles, which paled in comparison. The phrase NEGU has been dancing through my mind for all these months now, and it's really helped me to get through some very difficult days.

In His Amazing Grace,
Angela Robinett

Hi, my name is Rebecca. I'm thirteen years old.

Ever since my friend told me about this courageous, amazing girl named Jessica Joy Rees, I dreamed of meeting Jessie. Sometimes I feel like I have met Jessie because she has changed my life. She has inspired me to "Never Ever Give Up," and I never will! She is a wonderful girl. She made me want to be a better person, and ever since I visited the NEGU website, I knew I wanted to dedicate my time to charity.

I have often fallen asleep thinking about how much Jessie has made a difference, and when I wake up, I realize I have literally dreamed of stuffing JoyJars with Jessie. It breaks my heart to know I can't, but I know it broke a lot of people's hearts on January 5th. I also believe that Jessie is now an angel, even though she has been all along. When I prayed at night, of course, like many others, I just prayed for Jessie to get better. But then I realized we were all praying for her to have no pain, and it worked.

Please let me know if it is possible to help make JoyJars with the Rees family in honor of Jessie and all of the other amazing kids in the world.

Love,
Rebecca Stillman
I NEGU

I had planned the Celebration of Life service very carefully. I knew who I wanted to speak, who I wanted to perform, and which artist I wanted to paint pictures while the service went on. Tom Clark was an artist I knew through Saddleback. I didn't tell him what to paint. I trusted him enough to know that whatever he did would be perfect.

In the notice about the service, we asked people to dress in bright colors. Jessie would not have wanted people in all black. I wore my NEGU T-shirt with Jessie's signature — thou

I did wear a suit jacket over it—and many others wore their TeamNEGU shirts. I had asked the people who were speaking to type up their comments so that, in the event they were too emotional to speak, a "backup person" could read for them. I, too, had a backup person.

The stage was lined with JoyJars containing flowers. As the service started, I noticed that everyone was looking solemn, and the room fell quiet. Even with more than five thousand people in attendance, there was total silence.

"This is just way too silent for Jess, so turn to somebody and give them a hug," I started. After thanking them for attending, I told them, "Today we are going to do two things. We are going to celebrate Jessie, and we are going to celebrate Jesus."

Throughout the service, two singers and a band that included three kids from my best friend Jeff's family played the songs from Jessie's "fave" list on her iPad. They started with "I Can Only Imagine" by MercyMe, while Tom Clark set to work on his first oil painting—a heart in the middle of an angel's wings. A blank banner decorated the middle of the heart. He blocked in the basic shapes with brown paint, then set to work on the next painting—a dove in a nest. The third painting in the triptych would be two hands with a shining sun in the middle.

Youth pastor Kurt Johnson read three of Jessie's favorite verses, starting with Philippians 4:13, then Romans 15:13: "May the God of hope fill you with all joy and peace as you trust in him, so that you may overflow with hope by the power of the Holy Spirit." And Philippians 4:4–9:

> Rejoice in the Lord always. I will say it again: Rejoice! Let your gentleness be evident to all. The Lord is near. Do not be anxious about anything, but in every situation, by prayer and petition, with thanksgiving, present your

requests to God. And the peace of God, which transcends all understanding, will guard your hearts and your minds in Christ Jesus.

Finally, brothers and sisters, whatever is true, whatever is noble, whatever is right, whatever is pure, whatever is lovely, whatever is admirable—if anything is excellent or praiseworthy—think about such things. Whatever you have learned or received or heard from me, or seen in me—put it into practice. And the God of peace will be with you.

Papa spoke about Jessie's faith and her caring nature. "Gale Sayers wrote a book called *I Am Third*. God is first, family is second, and I am third," he said. "Jessie's book would be *I Am Fourth*. God is first, family is second, everyone else is third, and I am fourth."

Tanta spoke next about Jessie's love of music and how we were all searching for our "brighter days" now that Jessie had found hers in heaven. "In the music world I've often heard it said, 'I only use the good notes.' Jessie was all the good notes."

Jessie's fifth-grade teacher, Mrs. James, shared some fun memories: "At one point in the year, Jessie ended up sitting right next to my desk. Sitting next to the teacher is a unique place to be because there are things one sees and does that others may not. Jessie used to play little tricks on me by putting things of hers on my desk, which is usually way too full as it is. When I would notice it and pretend to be annoyed, she would giggle and grin—I loved that giggle and those amazing blue-gray eyes. She was the epitome of joy. I am so incredibly impressed with what she accomplished in so little time. Sweet Jessie angel, spread your wings. No longer think of scary things. Rise above the glistening sun. Your work on earth has just begun. He who began a good work in you will be faithful to complete it."

Jessie's best friend, Sophie, came to the podium in her NEGU shirt and her NEGU-studded headband, looking like a twelve-year-old girl but carrying a weighty grief that belied her age. She read her first two sentences before the tears came, too strong to speak through. I gave her a few moments before asking if she wanted me to read the rest. She nodded, and I'm not sure how I got through her beautiful words either: "We all hoped for a miracle, then when Jessie left us we all realized that Jessie was the miracle even before she got sick. I once posted something on Jessie's wall that read, 'Anyone can give up—it's the easiest thing in the world to do. But to hold on for so long when everyone would understand if you fell apart, now that's true strength.' "

One of the things haunting Sophie was a conversation back when they were both ten years old about what they wanted to be when they grew up. Sophie said she wanted to be a doctor, but when it was Jessie's turn to talk, playtime was over and they never finished the discussion. Sophie said she always felt Jessie was destined to do something great, but she never did learn what Jessie dreamed of doing with her life on that day.

Her friend Grant talked about Jessie's sense of humor—like when she convinced him to throw a water balloon at JT and toss him in the pool. "Jessie changed our world forever, and this is just the beginning. Jessie always said, 'Never ever give up.' If you all never ever give up, then Jessie's legacy will live on just like her love for every single person on earth."

Jessie's second cousin Jayden explained that she had always wanted to be a pediatric oncology nurse. She was currently in college studying nursing, and she talked about how Jessie had impacted not only her walk with God but also her career. "If I can put a smile on every child's face I help in the future, I'll consider that a very successful life. Over the last ten months, Jessie has impacted my life more than anybody has in the last eighteen years. She showed me how to live a selfless life rather than a selfish one. She showed me how life becomes so much better and brighter when you focus on the positives and don't dwell on the negatives. Most importantly, she has taught me that giving up is never an option."

Finally, Coach Bryan shared his stories about Jessie's bravery. "I watch many swimmers from a young age grow as individuals, work toward their goals, and face their fears, but none have turned the tables on me and become such an inspiration like Jessie has. When faced with an obstacle, I simply think 'NEGU.' Never Ever Give Up. That's what my girl Jessie does. I have to be strong like her. I have to be courageous like her. I have to put my fears aside and move forward, no matter how hard things become, like Jessie."

When everyone else was finished, I spoke about how I thought God had taught us three lessons through Jessie: to love compassionately, to laugh constantly, and to live courageously. "Because of her life, I'm confident last Thursday morning she heard her heavenly Father say, 'Well done, good and faithful little servant of mine! You have been so faithful with spreading my hope, joy, and love; I will put you in charge of many things here —like making heavenly JoyJars. Come and share my happiness! I'm so glad you are home now, my sweet girl.'

"Many years ago Jessie made the most important decision in life—she asked Jesus into her heart. Have you?"

I then invited Rick Warren to the stage, and he gave a sermon in which he talked about the perfection of heaven and how the only way to get there was through a relationship with Jesus.

"Do you know God the way Jessie did? If you don't, you need to start getting to know him tonight," Pastor Rick said.

Then he asked people to pray along with him, to invite God into their hearts, accepting Jesus as their Savior and asking f eternal life. Those who had never said this prayer before were asked to stand with their heads bowed while Pastor Rick said a blessing for them.

More than two hundred people stood up and committed their lives to Jesus that day.

In addition to the five thousand people who came to the service, another four thousand watched it online in real time, and countless others have watched it since then. How many others were saved because of Jessie?

I had thought my daughter's biggest impact on the world had to do with her JoyJars, but I started seeing something else that day—maybe it was part of the answer I was seeking. More than two hundred people had just been given a home in heaven because of Jessie. That's some legacy. She cared so much about helping people—what could be better than helping them have eternal life?

People had told me that in time, we would heal. We would start to forget and things would go back to normal, but I didn't ever want to forget. So at the end of the service, I prayed that we would never be the same again. "God, thank you for this celebration, and let it never end in our hearts. In Jesus' name. Amen."

The last song was Travis Ryan's "Fearless," and as the song began, Tom painted the thing we'd all been waiting for. In bold white paint, he wrote "NEGU" in the banner across the heart. Those three beautiful paintings, which spelled J-O-Y, now hang in our home.

After the service, we had a reception on the patio, serving the meal Jessie liked best—dessert. We had plentiful amounts of cookies, cupcakes, and candy in her honor. Somehow we all got through the service, but it still felt like a movie, like someone else's life. We stood out on the patio and got all sugared up and ved up, and all I could think was, *I wish Jessie was here.*

keeping faith

After Jessie went to heaven, many of us struggled with our faith. Nana and Papa felt completely betrayed.

"I don't understand," Nana said. "Jesus promised. The Bible says that we can ask Jesus for anything in his name, and he will do it. How could he not heal Jessie?"

I had recognized all along that Jessie would most likely not survive this cancer, but they had not. They had rejected that idea outright, and so when she passed, they felt blindsided.

Papa thought back to a time the year before Jessie's diagnosis when she was decorating sets for a school play and lost her favorite bubblegum watch. She had retraced her steps and realized she'd taken it off in the bathroom when she washed out her brushes, but it wasn't on the sink anymore and it hadn't been turned in to the school's Lost and Found. A group of younger kids had come through the bathroom after she had, so the only explanation she could figure was that one of them had taken i

"I'll buy you a new one," Papa had offered.

never ever give up

"It's okay, Papa," Jessie had said. "God must have decided someone else needed that watch more than I did."

How could God have let such a faithful servant suffer? How could he have taken away such a light in our world?

"Why couldn't he have given me the cancer instead and let her live?" Papa asked.

It was a hard road back to faith for both of them, with Nana deciding that if this was how God treated his children, then she didn't want to be one of his children. She didn't think there was a point in praying anymore. She had prayed so hard for ten months, and her prayer had not been fulfilled. Books about grieving didn't give her the answers she was seeking. It was a complete shift in what she'd been taught her whole life, and it was devastating. Not only had she lost her granddaughter and had to watch her children suffer so greatly, but her faith was shaken too.

Papa heard a sermon at Harvest Christian Fellowship in which Pastor Greg Laurie described an encounter with a parishioner who asked, "Do you ever get mad at God or not believe in him?"

"Sure I do," Pastor Greg said.

"Well, what do you do?"

"I change my mind because God is right."

Papa thought about that a lot. How could God be right in this case? What was "right" about Jessie's death? He felt very challenged, but he kept searching for answers in Scripture and in his heart.

He thought about several of the things I'd said—about how God doesn't owe us an explanation for his actions, and how we have to accept that his will may be different from our will. ıst because God hadn't answered our prayers in the way we ınted didn't mean he hadn't answered them at all: Jessie was fully healed, fully restored, in heaven. Her suffering was over, and she was cancer-free. That was what we had asked for—it just wasn't delivered in the same way we had wanted.

And although we were sad Jessie's life had ended so abruptly, I never felt cheated that she didn't make it as long as the doctors had originally predicted. It was a great relief that in the end, God didn't prolong her suffering. We didn't get our final warning signs, but that meant Jessie never went through the worst this disease has to offer. That in itself was an answer to prayer.

Nana and Papa thought about this over and over until they came to some sense of peace with it. We could not possibly know why God needed Jessie so soon, or what important lessons he intended to teach with her short life. We could make guesses, but we would not know until the time came for each of us to be with Jesus too.

Papa prayed one night, "God, you're God and I'm not. I know you don't owe me an answer, but I'd like to have a little understanding." Two days later in his Bible study, Papa read the passage in which Joseph says to his brothers in Genesis 50:20, "You intended to harm me, but God intended it for good to accomplish what is now being done, the saving of many lives."

Cancer intended to harm Jessie, Papa thought, *but look at all the good that has come of it since then.*

He thought about the two hundred people who had stood up to receive Christ at her Celebration of Life service.

He thought about the three thousand children Jessie had personally sent JoyJars to—and the thousands more who soon would receive one.

He thought about all the people who wrote to us to say they'd been inspired to do something good because of Jessie— small things, big things, all kinds of things that would improve the world.

He thought about the fans on Facebook—now more than 300,000 and growing rapidly—who would all now know more about DIPG and the need for a cure.

What was intended to harm Jessie, God intended for good, Papa thought. And he tattooed "Gen. 50:20" under Jessie's signature on his arm, along with "Phil. 4:3" and "Joshua 1:9" under JT's and Shaya's signatures.

There were so many times throughout Jessie's journey that I thought about the idea of choosing to be bitter or better. Jessie had clearly chosen to be better all throughout her fight. Stacey and I had to make that same decision at several points—when Jessie was diagnosed, when the second tumor appeared, and when she passed. At any of those points, we could have remained in bitterness, but to do so would not have honored Jessie. The only real choice was to be better. And that day, Papa chose to be better too.

Each day, he recited Psalm 139:23–34: "Search me, God, and know my heart; test me and know my anxious thoughts. See if there is any offensive way in me, and lead me in the way everlasting." As he recited it this time, he felt there *was* something offensive he had done, and he wanted to make it right.

Papa apologized to me.

He did not have to. I loved him like a dad. I understood well that everything he had said and done was with love, but in that moment, he realized it had been hurtful to tell me I wasn't praying enough, wasn't believing enough, for Jessie to be healed. All along, that's not what it had been about. It had been about God's will, not our will. God did not choose to take Jessie to heaven because I didn't pray enough, and we both realized that now.

"I am truly sorry," he told me. "You were up front about ie's disease from the beginning, and I didn't want to believe it. I was too forceful with my beliefs, and I think I caused the tensions in this family because of the way I spoke. I did it so I could 'believe without doubting' that Jesus would heal Jessie, and I was wrong in how I handled it."

Some families fall apart in times of extreme stress. We're trying to use this as an opportunity to grow closer. Misunderstandings can be fixed. Hurt feelings can be mended. It all comes down to love. When love is at the base of it all, there is always a way to work things through—and there is great love here.

* * *

There are times in all of our lives when our faith will be tested and challenged. This was obviously a time of extreme challenge for us. But as with anything that's truly in your heart, you'll find a way back to it. Nana realized Jessie would not want us to be unhappy and separated from God. Papa talks now about how he matured as a Christian because of this. Nearly seventy years old, he realized he still had things to learn about the faith he had carried all his life. And me, a pastor, still learning all the time and working hard to plant my feet in absolute trust in the Lord while my heart remains broken.

When people ask how I am, I usually tell them I feel "peacefully empty." Peaceful because I know Jessie is cancer-free in heaven, but empty because I wish she was still here with us. It never felt quite right when people would say they were sorry Jessie had died, so one day I said to a friend, "She's not gone. She's just moved to heaven." That's what I try to remember—that she may be too far away for me to see her right now, but she's happy in her new home.

Every Thursday since her passing, I write in my "Jessie Journal" online—letters to her telling her what we've been up to, how we're doing, and what I miss about her. At first, it was hard to write more than a few lines, but now I write pages sometimes, telling her all about the good we're doing in her name and the everyday things our family does. I told Jessie when we went back to Disneyland to celebrate Shaya's fifteenth birthday and when she got her braces off and made the varsity swimming team. I told her when JT was chosen to go to Clovis and that he kept saying he wished there was FaceTime in heaven. I told her about making red velvet cupcakes with cream cheese frosting on what would have been her thirteenth birthday.

Then there were the tougher things to tell her, like how much we were praying for Stacey on Mother's Day, a devastating holiday when one of your children isn't with you. I told her about how heartbreaking it was when strangers would ask simple, practical questions about how many kids I had — like when we were on a plane and the attendant wanted to know how many headphones we needed for the kids. "Two," I said, but it felt awful. "I have three kids," I wanted to tell him. "It's just that one of them is playing in heaven."

The first time we stayed in a hotel and ordered room service with those funny little ketchup jars, I told them we had three kids but only two were eating.

When we heard about any of our courageous NEGU kids losing their fight with cancer, I asked Jessie to welcome them to heaven and show them around. I pictured her running around with the dogs and surrounded by whole bakery racks full of sweets, sharing them with the children who had just arrived.

I prayed to God, asking him to let Jessie peek through the clouds and see us sometimes, but not when I was writing those journal entries. I cried so much writing them, and I didn't want her to see me like that. There were better times. I would have 	ed for her to see how much the community continued to rally 	nd us long after the service was over. I don't think we had to cook for three months. People brought us food and ran the errands we couldn't even think about early on. Papa's coworkers covered shifts for him whenever he needed. My friend Gerald came to the house to check on me and asked for my car keys. Then he took my car for an oil change and car wash and topped off my gas tank.

Tanta and Bob, whom we called the "silent force" because of the way they always stepped up without any fanfare when we needed a hand, realized how painful it would be for us to look every day at the couch where Jessie had passed, so they took us out to buy a new couch.

I thought about what it takes to overcome loss, and this acronym came to mind:

Letting
Others
Strengthen and
Support

The only reason Stacey and I got out of bed every day was that we had two other kids who needed us and deserved to have lives that weren't centered on grief. We didn't do it perfectly, but we did what we could each day. Our marriage will never be the same as it was before Jessie's cancer; that's just how it is. Our family will never be the same. We grieve differently, and sometimes it's hard to connect when we don't have the same ways of dealing with pain. We went to counseling and mourned separately and together, but we also tried to find the spirit to continue having happy times too.

It was hard to imagine taking a real vacation without Jessie, so we found a way to include her. We took a trip to New York that summer in time for Fashion Week and used lists Jessie had made on her laptop as our itinerary. There were particular sho and restaurants she'd wanted to visit, so we visited for her.

We watched the Olympics together, knowing full well how much Jessie had been looking forward to seeing them, particularly the swimming events. Sometimes we light the incense Jessie had loved from her acupuncture days or make the kinds of sweets she liked best.

Somehow we got through our first Christmas without Jessie. Stacey went with the motto "Go big or go home," getting a tree big enough for us to camp under. We put up all of Jessie's special ornaments and gave gifts from her. But the gift that everybody wanted—another Jessie hug, another Jessie laugh, Eskimo kisses, and another whispered "I love you"—couldn't be filled.

There are days when I still can't believe she's not going to come walking back through the front door. Once, I even called out over my shoulder, "Look both ways, Jess!" when I was crossing the street with JT. Such a tidal wave of grief hit me when I realized what I'd just said.

People think the first year is the hardest, but we've come to decide that the second year may be worse. Once you get through all the "firsts"—first Easter without her, first birthday, first Father's Day—then the reality starts to sink in. I think shock carried us through most of the first year, and then we were left with facing the rest of our lives.

"She's really not coming back," Shaya told us one day. "I'm never going to get to be her role model."

It took us more than a year to tell Shaya we had known all along that DIPG was nearly always terminal. It felt wrong to continue misleading her, so we told her—and asked if she thought we had done the right thing. She said yes.

"If you had told me from the beginning, I might have done some things differently, but it would have been a terrible year."

JT spoke eloquently to his classmates about Jessie and how would see her again in heaven. His teacher wrote to say how proud she was of how well he'd handled it. Both of the kids break down sometimes when they're missing their sister, but we're all doing our best to live each day well and not take anything for granted.

We all have both moments of happiness and moments when the pain swells up to a tipping point again. For me, it comes unexpectedly sometimes when I picture Jessie's eyes — those sparkling blue eyes that were so full of life and joy. We've replaced her bed with a couch now so we can sit in her room whenever we want to and reflect, and one of the things that gets me every time is seeing her glasses on the shelf. Those glasses with the silly Scotch tape over one lens. They make me picture her eyes again.

Recently, I was diagnosed with post-traumatic stress disorder (PTSD), the same affliction that affects many war veterans and involves symptoms such as hyperarousal, nightmares, and flashbacks. My doctor explained that it began as acute stress disorder when Jessie was first diagnosed — and I've learned that about half of all parents of children with cancer meet the criteria for acute stress disorder within two weeks of the child's diagnosis.

I'm sure some people go through the stages of grief in a neat and orderly fashion, but not us. It's been a roller coaster where some days I feel okay, and other days I'm mad at God again and questioning everything.

I will never know what my daughter would have been when she grew up. I won't know who she would have married, or watch her become a loving mother to her own children. Her framed class photo collage is empty after the sixth grade. And still I ask myself, *Why, God? Why Jessie? Why now?*

I know a boy who's had DIPG for three years already, and sometimes that even makes me mad. Why couldn't Jessie ha: had three years?

We cannot understand with our finite minds God's infinite plans. All we can do is to trust that when we are suffering, there is a greater cause. God doesn't let us suffer pointlessly. So when you're hurting and wondering why God isn't taking your pain away, consider that you're playing a role in a greater picture than you could ever imagine. I don't pretend to have all the answers, or even most of them. I don't know why he had to call Jessie home in the way he did, but time has given me clues about what her purpose may have been, and that enables me to keep my faith alive. I will see my daughter again in heaven—this I know. She will come running toward me and jump into my arms and say, "Welcome home, Daddy."

the jessie rees
foundation

We had that gala after all, just ten days after Jessie's memorial service. How did we do it? I don't know. It was almost unthinkably difficult to throw a big party so soon after Jessie's passing, but I couldn't imagine *not* doing it. All of Jessie's efforts had led up to this. It was a huge fund-raiser and a very meaningful one for the kids we served.

Since Jessie couldn't hand out medals of courage to the courageous kids fighting cancer, Shaya and JT filled that role. I gave out the awards to the teen volunteers who had made big contributions to our efforts. Ronnie took over emcee duties for the night to give me a break in that sense, but we were all there. We all danced and sang and cried for Jessie while we did our best to make her dream come true.

A fifteen-year-old boy named Austin Gatus who knew Jessie online had written a song inspired by her and offered to perform it for us at the gala. He wrote it shortly before Jessie went to heaven and she never got to hear it. He had hoped the would meet for the first time at the gala. Austin was a longti

pediatric cancer fighter himself, having survived acute lymphoblastic leukemia (ALL) after a grueling battle that included years
of treatments and surgeries.

Honestly, I thought it would just be a nice thing to give a
forum like that to a child who'd gone through cancer. I had no
idea he was going to be as talented as he was, or that his song
would be as beautiful as it was. Austin stood on the same stage
John Tesh had just stood on, alone with his acoustic guitar, and
gave a performance that brought the audience to their feet in a
standing ovation.

> *Never give up; it'll be okay*
> *Don't stop trying — there's a way*
> *Through the darkness and the rain*
> *Through the sorrow and the pain*
> *So don't lose hope, don't lose faith*
> *Keep on trying every day*
> *Never Ever Give Up.**

We raised $100,000 that day, but more importantly, we made
connections that would enable the foundation to soar. After the
gala, a man named Matt Davis said to me, "I want to pay your
foundation's rent for the next couple of years."

Pardon me?

What he was offering was a miracle for us — a real home for
the Joy Factory. It was an eighteen-thousand-square-foot ware-
house where we could spread out and keep all our supplies, hold
board meetings, and invite people to stuff JoyJars whenever they
wanted. When we were in the garage, we were much more limited, but now Girl Scout troops and TeamNEGU clubs would
have a place to get together to assemble JoyJars with us.

---

*"Never Ever Give Up," music and lyrics by Austin Gatus. Used by
permission.

Another man, whose name was Noah, had paid for a table at the gala for his family and friends, but at the last minute, he decided not to attend. He had two daughters, and it was too painful for him to imagine himself in my shoes. Thankfully, we were able to meet in person a few days later at a local Starbucks.

"Tell me how I can help. What do you need the most?"

"A staff," I said. "Right now, it's just me and our board of volunteers. We could really use funding to help us hire a few people to help us with office duties — mailings, inventory, event planning ..."

Two days later, Noah had met with some amazing people to share our vision and secured funding for us — $350,000, which would cover all our staff expenses for three years. It was astonishing. We hired four people to work in the Joy Factory.

We also asked four-time Olympic medalist Kaitlin Sandeno to be the national spokesperson for Jessie's foundation and to lead our NEGU All-Stars. She travels the country sharing Jessie's NEGU message while delivering JoyJars. Several other professional athletes join her to make special deliveries as well.

I'm sure many people expected Jessie's foundation to slow down or even stop once she had passed, but the opposite happened. It took off to heights we'd scarcely imagined before, and very quickly. I'd had a conversation once with Shaya and JT to make sure they were okay with it, because it meant a lot of our energy would still be spent focused on Jessie's mission and her memory, and I didn't want them to feel like they were being lost or forgotten in the process.

"No, the JoyJars *have* to continue," Shaya said.

"Yeah, we can't quit!" JT said.

With their blessing, I dove into the next chapter of our story. Considering that Jessie could no longer object, the board voted to rename the NEGU Foundation the Jessie Rees Foundation. All of this was in her memory, and I just didn't want the world to ever forget her name or what she started. We renamed it on April 8 — on what would have been Jessie's thirteenth birthday.

With our massive online following continuing to grow, we were easily able to win a grant, based on online voting, from NASCAR's five-time Sprint Cup Series champion Jimmie Johnson's foundation. We were one of two charities selected in 2012 to receive a $10,000 grant, as well as to have the name of our foundation featured on Jimmie's helmet during the Sprint Cup race in June. We also swept the votes to win a grant from the Orange County Community Foundation.

When the new school year started, some kids began TeamNEGU clubs in their high schools. A friend of Shaya's in her school was the first to organize a club, and Shaya gladly joined. Then the kids on our Junior Board of Directors started their own clubs. By October, there were five clubs, one of which had recruited more than fifty members. The kids and their faculty advisers helped us publicize our events, such as the swim meets, where we'd have a booth, and the golf classic. Most of the clubs met once a month, and they organized toy drives and ran fund-raisers to support the foundation. Our porch was often filled with boxes full of toys coming from drives like these.

A young woman named Alli Baker started her own crafty mission called "Butterflies for Courageous Kids," inspired by Jessie. She makes personalized paper butterflies and has mailed them out to kids fighting cancer and their siblings. She's now sent more than two thousand of them to kids in eight countries. Another wonderful lady named Cathy, who creates handmade jewelry, designed a silver NEGU pendant with a hand-stamped JoyJar on it and sent all the profits from its sales to the foundation.

In December, Jessie posthumously won a Young Wonder award from CNN, which was a very big deal. The award was presented at the annual "CNN Heroes: An All-Star Tribute" awards ceremony at the Shrine Auditorium in Los Angeles, hosted by Anderson Cooper. Ten Heroes and three Young Wonder awards were handed out, with presentations on a large screen to show the audience what each of the winners had done to earn their honors. Nearly a year after Jessie's passing, there she was, fifty feet tall on a huge screen, smiling and talking about her JoyJars. It brought us all to tears.

"What makes Jessie a Young Wonder is that she cares," I said. "In the midst of a world that says, 'Focus on yourself—it's all about you,' she said, 'No, it's not.'"

That was also the month that we sent out our fifty thousandth JoyJar. We made it just before 2012 drew to an end, with help from donations from Anthem Blue Cross and UPS. It was the number Jessie had always talked about—one for every kid fighting cancer in a U.S. hospital—but I knew we were nowhere near our finish line. It was no longer about just sending out toys; now it was about a real movement. What Jessie did was larger than JoyJars. She became a beacon of hope and strength for so many people, and now we carry on in her honor.

Stacey and I want the Jessie Rees Foundation to be a household name, like the Susan G. Komen Foundation. Just like the pink ribbons and Livestrong are so closely identified with their causes, I want NEGU to be an international symbol of hope for children fighting cancer. We will care until there's a cure.

I'm just one dad. One regular guy who comes from a modest background. My daughter was a quiet elementary school student who mostly did her best *not* to stand out. We were not celebrities, and yet look at what we've accomplished in such a short amount of time.

In 2012 we began sending out holiday and birthday JoyJars, in addition to our regular ones, and in 2013 we expanded to make "NEGU Power Packs"—items to decorate a bedroom or hospital room, from a NEGU pillowcase and blanket to a decorative cover for an IV bag. They even include a stuffed doggie named Moe with an "I'm a NEGU Kid" T-shirt. And we have a special volunteer who now offers personal portrait sketches to kids fighting cancer, and we send special memory canvases to families that have children in heaven.

What's more, we now have more than a thousand partners in our family support network. We create one-of-a-kind sports adventures for kids to meet their favorite players, and we offer kids special room makeovers.

We've stuffed and sent out more than 80,000 JoyJars to courageous kids in 260 children's hospitals, 175 Ronald McDonald Houses, and thousands of homes. We have reached kids in all 50 states and in 27 countries. We personalize the jars as much as we can, based on what we know about the kids—their age, interests, favorite color, and so on.

JoyJars are just the start of a relationship. There's so much more we want to do to care for kids with cancer and their families, from offering counseling services and help with expenses to creating a worldwide support network. Some of those things are already in the works as the movement keeps growing. Our second golf tournament attracted 50 percent more participants than the first, and our second gala was a star-studded event headlined by Sharif Iman. As I write this, we now have more than 300,000 Facebook fans, and they've done outstanding things to help draw attention to our cause. If you are not one of our fans yet, please Like us.

We also have more than one hundred professional athletes

on our All-Star team who visit kids in the hospital. Lots of people are helping us raise money for childhood cancer by hosting our special community fund-raiser we call "Courageous Cupcakes." We encourage people to "help take a bite out of childhood cancer." If you would like to host one of these, just go to www.jessie.org and sign up. In March 2014, American Airlines joined forces with us to help spread more joy to children around the world. They even stuffed more than five thousand special edition JoyJars at their global sales conference in May. Talk about a massive boost of joy!

It was a jolt of joy to see someone with a giant NEGU sign hamming it up for the cameras outside the *Good Morning America* show one morning. I've lost count now of how many people have gotten NEGU tattoos, or even shaved NEGU into the back of their hair. Our fans have helped get Jessie's JoyJars featured on Katie Couric's show during a segment about a wonderful teen group called Lion's Heart, and they've helped us spread the word to media outlets and celebrities internationally. We even recently had a television crew from an Italian news station come join us in the Joy Factory.

In June 2013, I traveled to the Nike world headquarters in Beaverton, Oregon, to talk with the top eighteen high school quarterbacks in America at a special skills camp called Elite 11, put on by Student Sports and ESPN. The day after I spoke with the players, we got to bring local courageous kids to meet the players and coaches. It was a very special day for everyone. ESPN included our involvement in the camp when the show aired on national TV.

After the camp ended, I flew to Sacramento to kick off the NEGU for Kids California Tour. Thanks to the support of Anthem Blue Cross, we dedicated the entire month of July to encouraging kids to Never Ever Give Up. The tour started in Sacramento and ended in San Diego twenty-six days later. During that time, we visited fourteen children's hospitals and saw more than three thousand children.

This has all been possible just because Jessie wanted to do something to make other kids happy. And this is what I want to ask of you: As you've read about Jessie's story, I sure hope that you got something from it. I hope you felt inspired by her. But when I set out to write this book, I did it with an important goal in mind. I didn't just want readers to put down the book at the end and say, "Jessie was a great kid." It is my fervent hope that everyone who reads this book will feel inspired enough to do something positive in Jessie's honor.

It doesn't need to have anything to do with JoyJars or children's cancer, though it can. What would mean a great deal to my family is if you would pick any cause that's important to you or any need you think you can fill, and get involved like Jessie did. She didn't wait for permission or instructions. She just thought to herself, *What can I do to make someone feel better today?* and she did it. That's exactly what I hope you will do too, because it matters. The only way things get better is when people like you decide to *make* things better.

Imagine if everyone asked themselves the same simple question Jessie did: "How can we help them?" What a wonderful world it would be.

> UNLESS someone like you
> cares a whole awful lot,
> nothing is going to get better.
> It's not.
> Dr. Seuss, *The Lorax*

Use your gifts and passions to guide you to do good, and you will live a blessed life. Keep hope alive in your heart, and help others do the same. Please help Jessie's life set off a tidal wave of compassion around the world.

And Never Ever Give Up.

I NEGU ... do you?

ouch! life hurts . . .
but God heals!

When I set out to write about my journey with Jessie, I had two main goals—increase awareness of childhood cancer and increase hope in people who are dealing with difficulties in their lives. Jessie's little message to "Never Ever Give Up" is all about grabbing hold of hope to keep pressing on, no matter what life throws at us.

As I look back over Jessie's ten-month fight, the one thing that kept our spirits up was *hope*. Hope that there was a 1 percent chance she could last five years. Hope that she could even live longer. Hope that if she lost her fight, we would see her again because of our faith in God.

Research shows that a person can go a few days without water and a few minutes without air. I believe a person can only go seconds without hope. If I didn't have the "hope of heaven" and believe with all my heart that I will see Jessie again, then life here on earth would have absolutely no purpose.

Thankfully, Jessie reminded us what the purpose of life is when she answered Lisa Sigell's question during the first CBS interview. Lisa asked, "Why don't you focus on yourself and make it all about you?" Jessie tearfully said, "Because that's not what life is about." Jessie knew life was not about personal success and getting everything you want. She knew the true purpose of life was loving God with all of her heart and loving others. That is why she had a burden for hospitalized children. She loved God, and that love for him motivated her to think beyond herself and reach out to help others in need. This is what life is about, and this is worth waking up for each and every day.

I have no idea what hurdles you are facing in life or the depth of the pain hidden deep in your heart, but God does. God loves you more than you know and wants to help you thrive in life rather than survive life. God can replace bitterness with peace, anger with joy, depression with determination, and hurt with hope. However, we need to ask him to help us.

The Bible clearly shows us God's deep love for us and his desire to help us. Psalm 147:3 reads, "He heals the broken-hearted and binds up their wounds."

Let me ask you two questions ...

1. Where does your heart hurt today?
2. Where has life wounded you?

No matter what your answer is to these questions, God already knows and wants to heal your broken heart and bind up your wounds. That is great news, friend. I truly hope you ask God to help you, so you, too, can live with peace in your heart, power in your mind, and purpose in your day.

Jessie used to say, "God, please help me." That is all you need to say. Four little words that have the power to increase your joy, your peace, and your love for others. You just need to believe that God loves you and deeply desires to heal your broken heart and bind up your wounds. Do you? Then ask him for help. Stop right now and ask God for help.

Did you? I'm going to assume you did ask God for help. Please send me an e-mail at erik@jessie.org so I can encourage you in your journey. We truly are better together!

With God's help we both can embrace each day with hope, joy, and love.

acknowledgments

From Erik Rees: I want to thank my Lord and Savior, Jesus Christ, for giving me the power and passion to be better and not bitter. I want to thank my amazing bride, Stacey, for her continued grace, love, and forgiveness. I'm honored to be your husband. To Shaya and JT, thanks for your unconditional love, hugs, and kisses. I'm so proud to be your daddy too. You inspire me every day to press on. To Nana, Papa, Kimmy, Uncle T, Tanta, and Bob, thanks for your outpouring of love and grace. Your arms of comfort and hearts of love were always wide-open for Jessie and remain open for us. To Jeff, Rick, and David, thanks for always being there when I needed you. To my writing partner, Jenna, thanks for handling Jessie's story with love, care, and exceptional skill. To all of Jessie's Facebook fans, known as NEGU Nation, thanks for loving my daughter and inspiring her to Never Ever Give Up! Lastly, a special thanks to Toni and Ronnie for helping me turn Jessie's wish into a global movement of hope, joy, and love. You are simply amazing people!

From Jenna Glatzer: Thank you to the Rees family for trusting me with this important story and for giving me glimpses into such a wonderful, loving family. Thank you to Cliff Gibbons for sharing Jessie's link and leading me to her. Thank you to Pat and Greg Alch and Lisa and Chris Fries for all the love and support. Thank you to my Sarina for being the kindest person I've ever met. You are more than I ever hoped for, and I will love you forever. Thank you, Jessie Rees, for inspiring me.

25 ways you can help a family with a child fighting cancer

So many people really want to help, but they don't know what to do. Asking, "How can I help?" or saying, "I'm here if you need me," probably won't get a real response. It's hard for people in crisis to tell you what they need. So it's better to offer specific things or to just go ahead and do them. Regular chores are often hard to complete when families are consumed with everything that accompanies a medical emergency.

Here are twenty-five particularly thoughtful things you can do for people:

1. Mow their lawn.
2. Offer to babysit the other kids while one goes to treatment or medical exams.
3. Fill up their car with gas, wash the car, and/or get the oil changed.
4. Provide meals and/or grocery items.
5. Offer to take family photos for them.
6. Have a garage sale to raise money for the family.

7. Buy fun hats for a child who is losing hair.

8. Plant flowers in their yard.

9. Offer to look after their pets or walk the dog.

10. Bring activity books, sticker books, magazines, and kids' books.

11. Write them a note to say you're thinking of them.

12. Offer to drive siblings to activities.

13. Offer to run errands—grocery shopping, dropping off dry cleaning, etc.

14. Clean the house or give them a gift certificate for cleaning services.

15. Bring them a "movie night" package—a DVD, microwave popcorn, and candy.

16. Decorate their lawn with encouraging signs.

17. Put up or take down holiday decorations.

18. Do yard work.

19. Promote their Facebook page or any events in their honor.

20. Take siblings out for a play day.

21. Organize a closet.

22. Help them sort through their mail so they don't lose track of their bills.

23. Offer to make phone calls to their friends and family with important updates.

24. Help them write thank-you notes.

25. Order silicone support bracelets or stickers.

See more suggestions at www.negu.org.

The Jessie Rees Foundation

The Jessie Rees Foundation is a global childhood cancer charity dedicated to ensuring that every child fighting cancer has the support and resources to Never Ever Give Up. The mission of this Foundation was inspired by twelve-year-old Jessie Rees in 2011, who during her own fight with cancer chose to encourage other kids who couldn't leave the hospital by providing them with filled JoyJars and her Never Ever Give Up message.

As of July 2014, the Jessie Rees Foundation has been able to reach more than 100,000 children in approximately 275 children's hospitals, 175 Ronald McDonald Houses, and 10,000 homes. The Foundation has encouraged kids in all 50 states and in 27 countries.

The five core programs that advance its mission are:

1 Encourage courageous kids to NEGU.
2 Assist courageous families to NEGU.
3 Rally communities to NEGU for courageous kids.
4 Mobilize All-Stars to NEGU for courageous kids.
5 Inspire the world to NEGU for courageous kids.

To embrace Jessie's mission and support courageous kids fighting cancer to Never Ever Give Up, please visit www.jessie.org.

JESSIE REES FOUNDATION